Pedagogical Documentation in Early Childhood

# Pedagogical Documentation *in* Early Childhood

## SHARING CHILDREN'S LEARNING AND TEACHERS' THINKING

Susan Stacey

**Redleaf Press**®
www.redleafpress.org
800-423-8309

Published by Redleaf Press
10 Yorkton Court
St. Paul, MN 55117
www.redleafpress.org

First edition 2015
Cover design by Percolator
Cover photographs/illustrations by Bethlehem Child Care
Interior design by Percolator
Typeset in Chaparral Pro
Interior photos by Susan Stacey
Printed in the United States of America

Library of Congress Cataloging-in-Publication Data

Stacey, Susan.
  Pedagogical documentation in early childhood : sharing children's
learning and teachers' thinking / Susan Stacey.
    pages cm
  Includes bibliographical references and index.
  ISBN 978-1-60554-391-8 (paperback)
1. Early childhood education. 2. Early childhood education--Curricula.
3. Student-centered learning. 4. Inquiry-based learning. 5. Reflective
  teaching. 6. Observation (Educational method) 7. Critical pedagogy. I.
  Title.
  LB1139.23.S73 2015
  372.21--dc23
                          2014040909

Printed on acid-free paper

*For my sister Sarah, who knows instinctively how
to be in the moment with young children*

# Contents

# Preface

Emergent curriculum is learning that begins with keen observation and listening for a child's agenda, followed by deep reflection, responses, and support from the child's educators. It allows for children and teachers to co-construct curriculum that is intentional and meaningful. The use of emergent, inquiry-based practices with young children continues to spread rapidly throughout the world. Much exploration of these approaches has taken place in North America, Europe, Asia, Australia, and New Zealand. This is heartening for those of us who have spent many years advocating for play-based, child-centered learning.

We have learned much about inquiry and project-based learning from our counterparts in Reggio Emilia, Italy. After the devastation of World War II, families and educators in this northern Italian town began developing thoughtful, creative, and inspiring approaches toward the education of young children. These approaches have led educators around the world to consider their image of the child and consider how they might reflect that image in their teaching practices. Over time, some educators have adapted approaches from Reggio Emilia for use in their own early childhood settings.

I suspect that many of us first became aware of pedagogical documentation—the practice of making children's and teachers' thinking and learning visible through graphic displays of photography, work samples, and text—when we examined the work coming out of Reggio Emilia. This documentation was, and continues to be, astoundingly insightful, beautifully presented, and thought provoking. It is no wonder that this work has captured our hearts, minds, and imaginations.

My first exposure to the documentation of children's work has stayed with me for more than twenty years. It occurred when I was on a study tour at the Model Early Learning Center (MELC), a preschool for three- to five-year-olds in Washington, DC, where founder and director Ann Lewin-Benham had been exploring the work of Reggio educators and their leaders. The educators at MELC had been collaborating on-site at their school with Amelia Gambetti, a pedagogical leader who was visiting from Reggio Emilia. Ms. Gambetti worked alongside the MELC educators as a master teacher for several months so that they could experience approaches from the Italian schools. At this time, I was the program coordinator at Peter Green Hall Children's Centre (PGHCC) in Halifax, Nova Scotia, and we too were immersed in the study of approaches and ideas from Reggio Emilia. The director of PGHCC, Barb Bigelow, and I were excited to hear that MELC was offering the opportunity through a study tour to view its environment and its work and to engage in dialogue with its teachers. We rushed to the phone to register for the tour!

We were not disappointed. Over two days, our thinking and learning about the Reggio Emilia approach to education deepened, and the experience challenged our assumptions. It was a rich learning experience on many levels. We viewed beautiful, thoughtfully planned environments that had been developed with intense attention to beauty, detail, and organization and with the child's possible actions in mind. We saw everyday items, such as mirrors, used in unusual ways. Natural materials and loose parts were plentiful. And we saw some equipment, such as light tables, that were new to us at that time. In addition, we viewed educators in thoughtful conversation with children, listening carefully and responding to what they heard. But it was during the first tour of the center that I came to a standstill, filled with curiosity and wonder. A simple documentation panel made me stop in my tracks. I turned to Barb and asked, "Have you seen this?" The photographs, precisely arranged in a horizontal format with text beneath each photo, told a story about an exploration of lines. The photographs, traces of children's work, and explanations provoked me to think about the children's thinking. But even more importantly, the very idea that inquiry and learning could be made visible in such a way stunned me. I had never before seen or heard of graphic representations of the collaboration between children and teachers. My first thought was "Of course! Why didn't I think of this before?" Demonstrating children's work in this way made perfect sense to me, and I wanted to try it—immediately.

Of course, the journey of learning to develop and use pedagogical documentation does not happen quickly. I had to invest some time, study, and experimentation before I was even remotely satisfied with a piece of documentation that I had produced. But the first piece that I tried upon returning from the study tour did have a profound effect on my colleagues at PGHCC. The piece was very simple: an account of a field trip to a pumpkin patch, together with the follow-up activities and conversations that happened in the subsequent days and a description of what the teachers believed the children had learned. This piece did not include the most awe-inspiring reflections, to be sure, but nevertheless it was a beginning. The teachers were delighted to see their work described. It seemed to me that they considered this documentation to be a validation of their work with children. It displayed the hard work, thought, and care with which the teachers developed curriculum. The children themselves were excited to revisit and talk about their experience. We were beginning a long-term relationship with pedagogical documentation.

Why does documentation resonate so deeply with us as teachers? Why, since it first appeared within early childhood settings in Europe and North America, have we embraced it with such vigor? When I ask educators about their thoughts on documentation, their responses almost always mention the way it makes them feel and the ways in which it provokes a response in others. Perhaps this is the most valuable aspect of thoughtful, well-executed documentation: regardless of its topic or format, it provokes a response—from other teachers, from families, and from the children themselves. Documentation at its best leads to reflection and dialogue. It also leads to decisions about development of curriculum and further research. It connects us to the actions of the children, to one another, and to the wider community. As educators, we are no longer working in isolation but are sharing our thoughts, our questions, our wonder, and the work of the children themselves. Sometimes we do not at first fully understand the meaning of the children's work. Questions arise, tangents develop, and our documentation becomes a story of our own attempts to understand and support children in their inquiry. Carol Anne Wien states:

> Pedagogical documentation is the teacher's story of the movement of children's understanding. The concept of learning in motion helps teachers, families, and policy makers grasp the idea that learning is provisional and dynamic; it may appear to expand and contract, rise, and even disappear. . . . Pedagogical documentation is a research story, built upon a question or inquiry "owned by" the teachers, children, or others, about the learning of children. (Wien, Guyevskey, and Berdoussis 2011, 2)

Pedagogical documentation supports us in our work. It provides a mirror that reflects our practice. When we view this mirror with an open mind and heart, it quickly becomes a tool for learning—not only for us and for children but also for families and other caregivers, who may wonder why we do things the way we do. Documentation can provide clarity when we look back at what has happened over the past few days or weeks. Typically, when children view themselves in action, they have something additional to say about what they did, and so the thinking and learning continues.

Over the years, I have introduced the idea of pedagogical documentation to many early childhood educators in North America. Participants in workshops and seminars have had the same reactions over and over again. They say that the documentation is beautiful, that it is a worthwhile endeavor, that it validates and tells the story of teachers' work and the work of young children, and that it has the potential to draw families into collaboration with teachers and children. However, challenges frequently arise when practitioners—whether they are students or seasoned educators—actually begin the journey of documenting children's work. Sometimes they underestimate the depth of reflection involved, and the text does not do justice to the children's thinking and ideas. Or practitioners working in busy classrooms simply cannot find the time to collect and assemble the necessary photographs, traces of children's work, and notes that are required for rich documentation. Yet for all the beginning struggles, many teachers persevere, practice and reflect, and produce wonderful narrations of what happened, the questions that arose, how they were investigated, and the roles of both children and teachers. Documentation, like the emergent and responsive curriculum it supports, is a journey, and it's one that's well worth the effort. This book is intended to support that effort, from beginning stages to the more sophisticated forms of documentation, and to clarify what documentation is and is not.

Let's take a look at the upcoming chapters and how this book can work for you. You will notice that every chapter ends with a section titled Invitation to Explore. Each chapter also contains ample photographic examples from real-life classroom work embedded within the text, so you can visualize how various forms of documentation might develop.

The introduction examines what pedagogical documentation is and is not, as well as why it is important for educators, children, and their families. We will think about teachers' reflection on their practice, professional growth, responsive decision making, and co-owning the curriculum with children. The introduction also offers a brief overview of the many types of documentation that are possible, with photographic examples. Finally, it discusses when and how each type is appropriate within the life of an early childhood classroom.

Chapter 1 addresses starting points: what we might document and where we might begin, with examples of documentation that began in various places within an inquiry or within the daily life of the classroom. In this chapter we will also take a look at the various stages of teacher development in using documentation. The chapter ends with an invitation to explore how we see children's thinking as it unfolds.

Chapter 2 explores the world of design and photography. Since high-quality documentation depends in part on how we present the photographs, notes, and children's work visually, we will turn to a design expert to learn about what works well and what gets in the way of a reader's viewing and understanding documentation. You will find practical suggestions for taking useful photographs and for choosing the ideal photographs for each piece of documentation. You simply cannot use them all! Also, we will examine the language that we use when describing children's work. How do we determine the essence of what is happening, and how do we clearly describe that? The Invitation to Explore at the end of this chapter involves making choices about photographs of children in action.

Chapter 3 provides a detailed deconstruction of some long-term projects, so that we can better understand the teachers' thinking as they made decisions about how to document the work. The Invitation to Explore asks you to reflect on these decisions.

Chapter 4 provides examples of the documentation of extraordinary moments—those seemingly small occurrences that crop up throughout the days with young children that provide flashes of insight for the child or the teacher. Although they are not part of long-term projects, they are nevertheless important for many reasons, which we will explore. The Invitation to Explore provides a chance to think and write about some extraordinary moments within your own classroom.

Chapter 5 takes a look at some creative ways of displaying documentation. We will examine formats, materials, and the use of odd spaces within the classroom, and we will celebrate the creativity of teachers who thought in unusual ways about physical spaces. This chapter invites you to consider your own environment and the potential within it for presenting documentation.

Chapter 6 takes a look at digital documentation, discussing both the advantages and the pitfalls. We will look at helpful applications and social media as a way of sharing with families and other educators, and examine what to consider when creating a blog or web page that uses pedagogical documentation. I will invite you to explore some high-quality websites that concentrate on documentation.

Chapter 7 provides a chance to look back and reflect on your practice and how the information within this book may support it. It introduces the idea of documentation as a form of teacher research, with an example. It also asks administrators and directors to think about their role in supporting pedagogical documentation. Finally, and importantly, in this chapter we will think about children's responses to documentation and how these responses can guide us as teachers. We will end with a final Invitation to Explore: What is next for you?

# Acknowledgments

Early childhood educators work hard to develop thoughtful, intentional programs for their young charges, often with little financial support or public recognition. Therefore, my first thanks go to those who work in this challenging and rewarding field, and who continue to seek out and embrace new and promising approaches to their work. These dedicated lifelong learners are to be applauded and admired, for they nurture the youngest among us at the most important times of their lives.

Those educators who have shared their work in this book have contributed to their field and to my own thinking and learning. They are Annette Comeau, whose design expertise was invaluable; Sandra Floyd, whose work inspired Ann Pelo to suggest that I reach out to Seattle to discuss Sandra's documentation; Donna Stapleton, who continues to lead her staff with creativity and dedication; Aya Saito, who, while still a student, challenged my own thinking to a deeper level; Susan Hagner, always a source of aesthetic and thoughtful environments for young children; and Leigh Ann Yuen, whose work with and documentation of toddlers reminds us of the deep capabilities of this age group. Many thanks to you all for your patience with this long writing and editing process and for your willingness to share your thinking.

Other thinkers have contributed greatly to my own learning: Margie Carter, Deb Curtis, and Ann Pelo all provoke my thinking each time we meet; Diane Kashin is the ultimate "sharer" through social media and therefore encourages us all to read about one another's work—even the work of those outside of our own field—and of course, my longtime mentors and friends Carol Anne Wien and Betty Jones are responsible, as ever, for stretching my thinking. Together with other friends and colleagues—including Liz Rogers, Liz Hicks, and Carrie Melsom—we have a group with whom we can bounce ideas around in a thought-provoking yet safe environment.

Much of the classroom work from Halifax Grammar School (HGS) would not have unfolded without my colleagues Martine Benson and Karen Cutcliffe, who were a part of the long- and short-term projects in the junior primary classroom. Linden Gray, head of the prep school, must also be thanked for her understanding of emergent curriculum and documentation and for the freedom she allowed me to explore new approaches.

Finally, a huge thank-you must go to the parents of the HGS junior primary children over the past five years. Not only did they demonstrate over and over again that they understood and valued our curriculum, but they also supported us in practical ways with materials, visits to the classroom to share expertise, and simply their overall trust and enthusiasm. I send them heartfelt thanks for allowing me to share their children's thinking and learning through this book.

# Introduction
## The What and the Why

## DESCRIBING PEDAGOGICAL DOCUMENTATION

When we notice and value children's ideas, thinking, questions, and theories about the world and then collect traces of their work (drawings, photographs of the children in action, and transcripts of their words) to share with a wider community, then we are documenting. However, several levels of documentation exist. The process of documentation becomes pedagogical—a study of the learning taking place—when we try to understand the underlying meaning of the children's actions and words, describing events in a way that makes our documentation a tool for collaboration, further learning, teacher research, and curriculum development. Carol Anne Wien provides insight into pedagogical documentation, stating that

> conceptualizing pedagogical documentation as teacher research calls upon the teacher not to know with certainty but instead to wonder, to inquire with grace into some temporary state of mind and feeling in children. (Wien, Guyevskey, and Berdoussis 2011, 2)

The process of documentation is indeed just that: a process, rather than simply a display. We watch and listen carefully, paying attention not only to children's play but also to their interactions with each other and with adults and to how they are using materials and their physical environment. In other words, we notice the ways in which the children relate with their world and what they think about that world. They may demonstrate their thinking through words, physical action, art, music, drama, and all the other ways in which children communicate their ideas—their "hundred languages" (Malaguzzi 1993). Therefore, we must be careful observers. We must also be discreet, so we do not interfere with their interactions.

If we have been taking notes and photographs, then we have information on which we can reflect. In a busy classroom, it may be tempting to omit the step of reflection. When we skip this step, it becomes "the missing middle" (Stacey 2009, 66), that is, the all-important pause to reflect that informs our practice. It is difficult

1

to find the time to meet with others in order to reflect together and engage in dialogue. But this is a crucial part of making sense of what children are doing. It helps us decide what we should pay deeper attention to, what we should respond to, and what we should document. In dialogue with our team or our mentors, we share our thoughts, test our theories, and ask each other, "What do you wonder?"

One of the most gratifying results of documenting children's work is that it supports our growth as teachers in many ways:

- It demands that we reflect upon our own practices. When a child has used materials or interacted with others in unexpected ways, when she struggles to bring her ideas to fruition, or when she passionately returns to her project day after day, pedagogical documentation forces us to ask ourselves questions: What is her intent? How can we support her learning? What prior knowledge or experience led to this discovery? What does this mean in terms of what we do tomorrow or next week? If we are to document the child's thinking or learning respectfully and with insight, we need to reflect on these types of questions.

- When we examine our data—photographs, notes, and recordings—we can then engage in intentional practice. Having observed, recorded, and reflected, we can make carefully crafted decisions about how to respond to the child. Perhaps we have a vast quantity of information and must carefully consider what, exactly, is important to respond to—and when—for we cannot respond to everything we see. When we tease out what we consider to be important for a child and put this together into a documentation panel or page, the process often leads us to next steps.

- In this way, curriculum becomes a collaboration between children and educators. And when we share pedagogical documentation with children, giving them an opportunity for further response, we become co-owners of the curriculum. How the children respond—what they say, what they notice, how they engage with the documentation—will inform our decisions about what to do next.

Ann Pelo, Margie Carter, and Deb Curtis describe this type of thinking and responding in Carter and Curtis's (2010) book, *The Visionary Director*, calling it "A Thinking Lens for Reflection and Inquiry®":

Knowing Yourself

Examining the Physical/Social/Emotional Environment

Seeking the Child's Point of View

Finding the Details that Engage Your Heart and Mind

Expanding Perspectives through Collaboration and Research

Considering Opportunities and Possibilities for Next Steps

These six points remind us to pay attention to our emotional responses to each moment with children, to keep our values in mind, to think about the children's thinking, to collaborate with others, and to reflect before we take action.

When we think about the cycle of inquiry—observing, reflecting, documenting, sharing, and responding—we can see that pedagogical documentation has the capacity to inform our classroom life in profound ways. It can influence children's and teachers' learning together and contribute to the development of a truly responsive curriculum. Documentation becomes so much more than display.

## THE NEED FOR SUPPORT

When directors ask early years practitioners to observe and reflect and then to produce documentation that demonstrates children's thinking and learning, they are asking for a commitment of time and mental energy. What can they offer to support this type of practice? While everyone may recognize the value of reflective practice and pedagogical documentation, along with all the intrinsic rewards that come along with this type of work, how can directors support educators in the practical sense?

Time is the most valuable resource that directors can offer. It is also the most difficult to provide. It takes time to reflect and to construct documentation. Directors struggle with providing this time. It costs money, since it requires coverage within the classroom. Here are some strategies that directors have shared with me:

- Share and reflect during staff meetings, instead of addressing business agenda items that can be managed through other forms of communication. When regular staff meetings become a time for sharing documentation and thinking together, they help staff form a supportive community of practitioners who think together. *[handwritten: Embedded collaboration Staff Meetings]*

- Provide the resources for educators to produce documentation *with* children, in the classroom. The concrete supplies must be on hand, well organized, and accessible at all times. *[handwritten: Set up w/ materials]*

- When longer pieces of documentation need to be produced, redistribute staff on low-attendance days in order to give one person time outside of the classroom to focus on assembling the data and mounting it.

- Employ other staff in constructing documentation. One director shared that when she was hiring a new administrative assistant/receptionist, she chose someone with an early childhood background, rather than an administrative person. One of the responsibilities of the new position was to construct documentation after meeting with the teachers in order to fully understand the described event. An assistant director or program coordinator can also fill this role.

- Keep expectations realistic. When we love documenting, we don't mind spending our own time to produce it. It is a pleasure for some educators to engage in this type of work. However, when we lead full lives both at work and at home, we sometimes just run out of time. We must keep our documentation simple so that it actually happens. It's better to have short, thoughtful, and simple pieces of documentation on a regular basis than to have none at all. Short pieces of documentation, more easily produced, can often be linked to form a larger and richer whole over time.

## THE MANY FACES OF DOCUMENTATION

Documentation comes in many forms. To find your own voice for documentation purposes, use those layouts and styles that best suit your children, families, and settings. Perhaps you are in an early childhood education community that values explanation of what you are doing and why. You would then put a heavier emphasis on text in your documentation. Or you might have a group of four- and five-year-olds who have plenty to say about their work when they see it documented. You might then put more emphasis on photography and tell their story in pictures as well as text that includes their dialogue. Maybe you have a group of parents who spend more time reading documentation when it is filled with children's work. In this case, you should ensure that your documentation always contains traces of that work. Or perhaps your observations of children lead to more questions for teachers, and your documentation becomes a narrative of how those questions were pursued as a form of teacher research to be shared with colleagues. Often, pedagogical documentation includes all these aspects.

We often admire and become inspired by documentation from other settings. In this digital age, it's easy—and helpful—to peruse the work of others. Yet, our documentation should be just that: ours. It should reflect our voices, cultures, and beliefs, and most importantly, the children within our particular settings.

As I described in the preface, my first viewing of pedagogical documentation occurred when I encountered a documentation panel that was put together by the educators at the Model Early Learning Center in Washington, DC. Their influences came from Reggio Emilia—a promising source, to be sure, in that the Italian educators provide such high-quality and insightful documentation. When I returned to Halifax, I spent several hours on my hands and knees with a T-square and spray adhesive before realizing that for the time being, I needed to keep things simple. A rich and complex story can be simply and still powerfully told.

Following are just a few of the options for documenting children's work. We will explore these options through detailed examples in later chapters.

## Documentation Panels

Documentation panels consist of photographs, text, and children's work mounted on foam board, Bristol board, or another sturdy surface. These panels can describe long- or short-term projects or processes in which the children are engaged. You might choose to create one panel or several panels that connect pieces of the story over a period of time.

## Extraordinary Moments

Small yet wonderful moments of learning unfold around us every day. You might use a smaller page or panel to describe such individual moments. This type of documentation consists of a simple paragraph or two of text plus one or two photos to support the readers' understanding. You can either display extraordinary moments or place them in a child's portfolio for sharing with the child and her family.

After noticing birds arriving at our bird feeder, several children pulled up "reading baskets" (laundry baskets), gathered clipboards, and sat in the baskets for more than a half hour, watching and counting birds and tallying how many visited. We teachers noticed that the counting had a competetive edge: who would see the most birds? We wondered, what is the importance of bird watching for these children?

## Daily Log

My own experiences have shown me that a daily log of some sort is an invaluable tool for communicating with families. Producing one page per day for a log takes little time, yet this small investment brings big rewards. It gives families a touch point to examine and talk about with their child. A daily log page contains a description and photo of only one or two moments during the day, but it transmits the flavor of the children's investigations. In the junior primary program at Halifax Grammar School, we placed our daily log on a small table just outside our door. Parents browsed through it with their children at departure time. Younger siblings also loved to look at this book, as did older students in our school who were just passing by.

## Documentation Developed by or with the Children

Whenever I sit down at a classroom table to do some on-the-spot documentation during the school day, curious children immediately surround me. This tells me some-

thing. They love to see their work, they love to see photographs of themselves working, and they love to see their work validated. They have plenty to say as I mount the photos and handwrite the text. So I have to adjust the words as we go. It is a fluid, organic process. The process helps me get a deeper sense of what happened, and it fascinates the children because they are seeing their own thinking made visible.

## Individual Portfolios

Many child care centers, preschools, and junior and senior kindergarten programs develop portfolios for individual children. Often, teachers use these portfolios for assessment purposes. They might include checklists or progress notes. However, a portfolio can *show* as well as tell a child's developmental story. Pieces of documentation can reflect the child's involvement in project work and complex play in various areas of the room. And transcripts of conversations with others can demonstrate understanding of a concept or a certain theory about the world. When a portfolio includes such documentation, it becomes much more than an assessment tool. It is also a story of ideas, investigations, and learning.

L. enjoys examining his own portfolio, remembering activities and understandings from past classroom life.

## Electronic Documentation

Depending on the type of setting in which you work, you may have opportunities to use applications to develop digital documentation and to disseminate this information electronically. This approach can make producing documentation incredibly convenient and quick. Some families may be more inclined to read the documentation if it appears on their smartphones or tablets. In addition, presentation applications such as PowerPoint can guide you through graphic design decisions and help you make your documentation look neat and professional.

However, electronic documentation does have its pitfalls. When your documentation process speeds up, you can find yourself with a missing middle if you skip the all-important step of reflection. We will explore this challenge in chapter 6, which discusses electronic documentation in depth.

## Transcripts or Recordings of Conversations

A conversation with a child can provide so much information about the child's ideas and way of thinking that you simply can't write it all down. This is when you need a recording device. If you record a child speaking, you can listen to the recording later, when you have a few free moments, and think about what meaning you should pull from the child's words. When you transcribe parts of these conversations and use them in documentation, you provide insight for others to consider, and the documentation itself becomes richer.

In the monograph *Making Teaching Visible*, Harvard Graduate School of Education researchers comment on this richness. They offer the example of conversations during and after a simple field trip:

> Consider the following: What if teachers kept track of what the children were saying on the trip, or alternatively, on coming back from the outing asked children, "What surprised you at the pond? What discoveries did you make?" The children's words (or writing or pictorial depictions) would add further information about the experience. What if the teacher were to add his or her perspective on the field trip, writing not only a log of what happened, but also an analysis of what learning and discoveries were made during the outing? The result would be a powerful reminder, not only of the events of the trip but also of the learning that happened as a result of the experience. Children would be enabled to reflect on their learning and potentially learn more. (Project Zero 2003, 54)

This quote reminds us to listen and take note, as well as watch. And then, we need to reflect on next steps.

## Learning Stories

Developed by Margaret Carr and Wendy Lee, both of New Zealand, learning stories are narratives that describe learning and help children see themselves as powerful learners. The primary audience for a learning story is the child herself and her family. Therefore, the narrative is written for and to the child. Here is a short excerpt, providing an example of the tone and vocabulary used in a learning story, provided by Louise Jupp, author of *Technology-Rich Inquiry-Based Research*, a blog that she publishes with Diane Kashin:

> J. and M., I noticed how thoughtfully you negotiated a fair plan to gather the beans from the garden together. You helped one another with the task and showed a great deal of co-operation and understanding of each other's ideas for completing the task. (Jupp 2013)

## The Classroom as Documentation

When thinking about the big picture of documentation—all that it entails, and the many ways in which it can be shared—it is important to remember that classrooms themselves are a form of documentation. For instance, what can we learn about someone else's philosophy, teaching approaches, and beliefs when we first walk into that person's room? We often form a strong first impression, then follow up with deeper browsing, a searching for links to the person's thinking and how the person makes that thinking visible. Each teaching and learning space has an ambience and a message, and we intuitively pick up on this message.

Room arrangement and materials send a message. Is the environment child-centered? What is the role of natural materials? What is the evidence of this space belonging to the children?

The walls send yet another powerful message: How and where is the documentation placed? Can the children see it clearly, in order to comment further on past experiences?

How are teachers collecting traces of children's thinking and ideas? Do they have note-taking systems? Are cameras on hand? Do the children themselves make decisions about what to share or what not to share?

Rather than serving as a way to judge, these types of observations can lead us to understanding the many ways that early childhood settings, and in particular their documentation, work to support the children. We can learn from the walls and the rooms of our colleagues.

Using pedagogical documentation, we can do much more than display what has happened in our learning environment. We can dig deeper, searching for the underlying motivations and ideas that the children are developing. We can comment on this analysis from the teacher's perspective, bringing families and other interested readers into the complex circle of thinking that is teaching.

## INVITATION TO EXPLORE

- How does the description of pedagogical documentation in this introduction compare or contrast with your previous understanding of documentation?

- If you have already begun documenting children's work, examine some of these pieces using a reflective lens. How does the documentation help you grasp the children's understandings or misunderstandings? If it does not help you comprehend their thinking, then what do you need to add?

# Starting Points

What do you envision when you imagine a typical day in your early childhood setting? Perhaps you think about all the activities, both planned and unexpected, in which the children are engaged: play, meetings, group times, special events, outdoor explorations, and so on. Or perhaps you imagine routines such as arrival, snacktime, transitions, rest time, caring for animals or plants, organizing the environment, and departure. There is so much going on within a rich program that when it comes to children's thinking, questions, and actions, it can be challenging just to decide what would be appropriate to document. How do we make these decisions? Why do we choose to document one event over another? In this chapter, we will explore possible starting points for documentation.

## WHAT ARE WE REALLY SEEING? THOUGHTS ON THE NATURE OF OBSERVING

Documentation begins with observation. But the word *observation* is a bit simplistic. When we are documenting children's learning, we are not simply watching and immediately responding with some sort of idea or decision. Rather, we are watching and listening with an acute awareness of how young children express their ideas and questions. These ideas and the ways in which children state or demonstrate them are often unorthodox from an adult point of view. So we must learn to listen and see in a way that is active and insightful—through a "thinking lens." Observing with a thinking lens means using our knowledge of recent events or experiences within the classroom, together with an understanding of a child's prior knowledge about the topic, cultural background, and family experiences, to understand where the child's idea, passion, or action is coming from. In other words, our observations must draw upon our relationships with children in order to make decisions.

We ask ourselves, considering all that we know about these children, what it is that they are attempting to understand or do. We are trying to arrive at meaning, or the underlying intentions of the children. Reflecting in this way helps us decide what is important to document. This documentation, in turn, informs our classroom practices. We follow a cycle of observation, reflection, documentation, and decision making.

## Drawing from Conversations with Children

The meaning behind a child's actions is rarely plain. Here are some examples of conversations and actions that seem simple on the surface. But when we reflect on them, we find that they hold interesting possibilities for the teacher and child's future work together. These possibilities might not have been recognized at first glance:

- A classroom toilet overflows, and the children are both fascinated and worried. They ask, "Why does it always do that?" They look under the sinks to see where the pipes go. They seem unaware that the toilet tank lid can be removed to see inside. But when asked by a teacher, they do know that "pipes take the yucky water away."

- During a reading of *Knuffle Bunny* by Mo Willems, the children notice that the backgrounds of the illustrations are produced with photography. They discuss this method of illustrating, and one child definitively states, "Photography is *not* an art!" This leads to many conversations, over days, about what does constitute art, and the children's opinions are varied.

## Beginning with Teachers' Questions

When we hear such comments from children, we often find ourselves formulating a question. In the cases outlined above, for instance, our questions were:

- How do children find out about how their homes and cities work? Where do their ideas and prior knowledge originate? What opportunities are available for further investigation of cleaning up our water? Are the children aware of this issue from an environmental point of view (perhaps through their families), or is this a practical puzzle about where water goes when it disappears from our homes?

- What are the children's thoughts on what constitutes art? Can their ideas about art be broadened? How could we do this without leading children toward the teachers' understandings of art? How could we encourage children to form their own ideas? Are there opportunities for developing multiple perspectives?

A teacher's question is a perfect place to begin documenting. A question creates the opportunity to frame the documentation as a response to this query—as a way of researching the answer. Following is an example showing how documentation unfolded in our classroom in response to the children's thoughts about art. We decided, after reflection, to pursue the idea of offering multiple perspectives of art, including using the camera as an art tool. This seemed to us to be a way of broadening children's knowledge without imposing our own ideas about art.

The children think about the art question during morning meeting. Their body language demonstrates their deep engagement in this question.

Alternate forms of art—including sculpture and music—were offered for consideration. Are these art? The consensus was yes. "Somebody made these with tools, but when you take a photograph, you just push a button." This comment from a four-year-old clearly explains his point of view: that art involves doing something with tools or materials rather than pushing a button. Although some adults may not agree with this statement, it opens up a door for exploration.

Cameras are put into the hands of children, and a studio is developed for dramatic play. What will they photograph? Will creative approaches appear? This is an invitation, and we cannot anticipate the results. Rather, we watch and wait.

We see through this short piece of documentation taken from a much longer whole how the documentation provided a kind of road map for the teachers. At each point, we were able to ask ourselves, "How did they respond to this? What does this mean?" After this investigation of art media and photography, we felt that the children were in a better position to think about art through a wider frame of reference. After weeks of investigating varied art media and using cameras in many ways, a visit from a photographer was arranged. She told the children, "My camera is my paintbrush." To this the children responded, "Well, *maybe* photography is an art."

## Tracking a Long-Term Project or Shorter-Term Investigation

Whether your children are working on one long-term project or several shorter-term investigations, you have many opportunities to track the journey through documentation. Documentation can help you keep families apprised of what is going on within the study and possibly enlist their input. It is important to share the documentation with children so they can see all the valuable work they have done, witness themselves in action (through video or photographs), and think—aloud, we hope!—about what they have discovered and understood, what questions remain for them, and what might come next.

Here is an excerpt from a long-term project on the human body that we documented and regularly shared with the children and their parents:

After observing children's struggles with making a standing human figure out of clay, teachers asked them, "Well, how do *we* manage to stand?" The children responded, "Muscles and bones!" Thus began a heightened interest in how the human body works. Many types of research were involved, including visits to the school library, where the librarian was always able to find appropriate books for our children to explore.

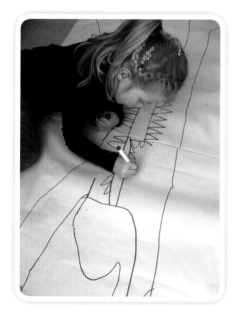

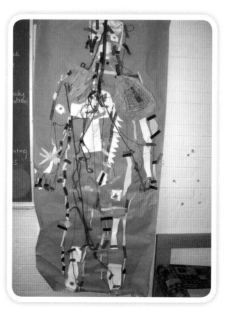

At each stage of this investigation, teachers invited children to draw their theories and ideas. Slowly, over a period of weeks, children added body parts to whole-body tracings, beginning with the skeletal system and progressing to organs, veins, skin, and so on.

Germs became a subject for more investigation due to the children's intense interest and their experiences with childhood illnesses. Children made germs from plastic modeling clay and also drew and painted on them, making comments such as "This is a chicken pox germ" and "This is a fever germ," thus demonstrating their understanding that specific germs lead to specific illnesses.

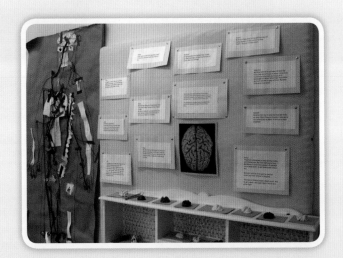

The study of the brain became a small project in itself. The children proposed theories about how brains send messages ("It goes down your arm to your fingers.") as well as what a brain looks like ("It's all wiggly inside."). Clay provided a way for children to represent the brain, and teachers wrote down their words about the "brain's job."

## Describing a Process

On occasion, you may find it necessary or worthwhile to explain to others—perhaps parents or student teachers—the processes that are underway in the classroom and why these processes are important for young children's development. For instance, do we all understand why cutting and assembling a collage of many bits and pieces is often included in early childhood programs? Do we agree that art should be process based? Why do we not worry about product? Why do we have morning meetings or circle times? And within those large-group meetings, what is happening for the children in terms of their social interactions, sharing of ideas, and learning?

The wonderful thing about these types of reflections and sharing of rationales is that they force us to examine why we do what we do! Through attempting to explain a process to others, many educators have changed their approaches because they realize that they have been following an old and perhaps outdated script that they inherited or that they no longer feel is valid. Others find that yes indeed, they want to keep a certain process or approach within their classroom, and within documentation they find a way to explain why.

## Examining the Children's Work Itself

Sometimes, even without special conversations, photographs, or notes, a piece of work—whether a model, painting, or piece of experimental print—is intriguing in itself. We may look at a piece of work by a child and think to ourselves, "That's interesting!" or "I wonder what this is about." And so, the work itself is what leads us to more questions, observations, and perhaps follow-up responses.

In what ways might we find a piece of work intriguing? Here is a brief example:

### K. and the Three Little Pigs

When K. joined us in our junior primary classroom at the age of four, she had never been in an early childhood program before. She did not speak English, except for a few necessary words to get through the day. Of course, she found her first weeks of school quite challenging, and she spoke very little as she observed what was going on around her and absorbed the English language. Although K. played alongside other children, we couldn't have significant conversations with her due to the language barrier. However, we did read to her in English—a lot!

One day, immediately after hearing the story of the Three Little Pigs for about the third time, K. went straight to the easel with a purposeful expression on her face. I couldn't interact with her at the time, but I watched from a distance as she painted slowly and intentionally. When she seemed to be nearing the end of her painting, I approached and examined the work carefully. It was astonishingly detailed. I wondered what it was about, so I asked her to tell me.

For a few minutes, K. used the vocabulary from the story reading to explain her painting: "The bad wolf, he is coming. The one little pig, he run. Here is the straw house." She gestured. "He huff and puff. The two little pig, they run. To the wood house. Here it is!" She pointed. "The bad wolf come and huff and puff. The three pig run to the brick house. He huff and puff but it no blow down! He fall down the chimney and run away."

These words from K. were, for us, a clear indicator that a child learning a second language could indeed learn the conventions and vocabulary of a new language from repeated storytelling, and that K. certainly understood how the story unfolded. Her painting provided the format and the confidence for retelling the story verbally. How did we document this for K. and her family? This small extraordinary moment is shown through documentation here.

K. demonstrates a sense of story through her painting and dictation, using a beginning, middle, and end as well as characters and quotes from the old tale of the Three Little Pigs. It seems that painting the story has become a type of visual language for K., one that supports her spoken words. While she was working on this painting (which took about twenty minutes), K. was intensely focused, often pausing to think before moving on to the next aspect of the work, demonstrating her intentionality.

## TEACHER PROGRESSIONS IN LEARNING TO DOCUMENT

We all come to early childhood education from different backgrounds, with different levels of education and varied experiences. So it is not surprising that pedagogical documentation is also very varied and that to some extent it reflects the practitioner through the way in which she selects topics, interprets actions, and presents physical artifacts.

Carol Anne Wien, my colleague and mentor for many years, has formed a theory about how teachers develop as documenters. Like any skill, documentation must be learned. It begins with simple steps that progress to an increasingly sophisticated practice. Wien suggests that teachers move through the following progressions as they learn to document:

1. developing habits of documentation

2. becoming comfortable with public recounting of activities

3. developing visual literacy skills

4. conceptualizing the purpose of documentation as making learning visible

5. sharing visible theories for interpretation purposes and further curriculum design (Wien, Guyevskey, and Berdoussis 2011, 4)

Let's take a look at how these progressions play out within the classroom. Here are some examples from my own classroom and from others I have visited.

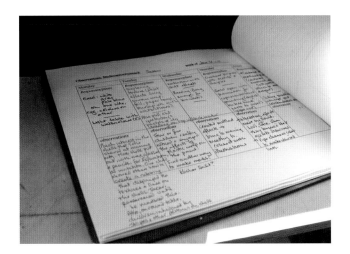
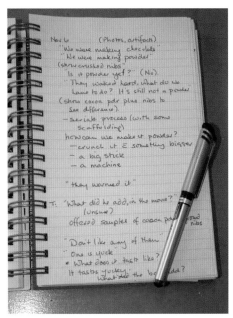

## Developing Habits of Documentation

To collect data to use for documentation, we must have an organized and efficient system. Otherwise notes become lost, photos fill up our cameras' memory cards, and we spend too much valuable time seeking information. We have several options for organizing our observations: arranging clipboards around the room, making electronic notes on a tablet, using sticky notes in a central, easily accessible location, or keeping a central logbook to which all members of the team contribute.

Which form of organization we choose as teams or individuals depends in part on what suits our dispositions and our levels of neatness. What will it take to get you to reach out and find a note or photo when you need it? How much space do you have on your countertop or desk? Are you the kind of person who needs a note-taking method close at hand all the time, or will you walk to another part of the room in order to write? These seemingly small, practical details matter in the course of a busy day. We must make it easy for ourselves to document, or it will not happen.

## Becoming Comfortable with Public Recounting of Activities

What is your comfort level with going public? Would you prefer to begin by keeping your documentation within the classroom or in a hallway within your center or school? Or are you quite confident with sharing online, perhaps through a blog? There are degrees of going public, and you need not share with the wider world if you do not feel ready to do so. If your documentation makes a statement about what you think is happening and why, it takes confidence to put such thoughts out there in the public domain.

When you share written work, it must, of course, be grammatically correct. Your documentation must also be understandable to others. Therefore, it is useful to get feedback from a trusted colleague. Can your colleague spot errors in spelling? Does your colleague understand the point of the work, or is your colleague reading something else into the photos and text that you have provided? Documentation is an act of communication. When you go public, you must ensure that the message you think you are sending is the message others are receiving.

## Developing Visual Literacy Skills

How documentation appears to others is important. It must be appealing enough to

A student teacher's documentation assignment with events thoughtfully connected through a time line.

draw people in without being cluttered. Text must be in a size that is readable to the observer. Photos must be clear and engaging. And above all, the flow of the visual must be logical, so that the reader can make sense of what to look at first and where the eye should travel. For instance, in Western cultures, our eyes move from top to bottom and left to right as we read. Although not all documentation must be set up in this linear fashion, *how* people are likely to engage with the visuals must be considered. In chapter 2, a graphic designer will explain the importance of giving readers a "resting place" for their eyes, so that a piece is not too visually stimulating.

You can learn visual literacy skills from a graphic designer, by reading and studying, or from workshops offered in your area. In addition, you may find inspiration from websites with high-quality documentation. When you find a design that you like, ask yourself why it attracts you. Is it because it is visually easy to follow? Is the text meaningful yet easy to understand? Is it beautiful to look at? Is it simple and uncluttered? Does it incorporate all of these factors? When you're learning about design, it's helpful to look at many examples of documentation while reflecting on what does and doesn't work for you as a reader.

## Conceptualizing the Purpose of Documentation as Making Learning Visible

Pedagogical documentation is not about making a pretty display or using photographs that are cute. These approaches do not do justice to the child's thinking, curiosity, and competence. Ann Lewin-Benham, in her book *Twelve Best Practices for Early Childhood Education* (2011), reminds us that "documenters' intentional recording makes it possible to reflect on past experiences, to extract meaning, and to project the meaning onto future experiences" (108).

## Sharing Visible Theories for Interpretation Purposes and Further Curriculum Design

Over time, experienced documenters can make visible their theories about children's intentions, about why and how these intentions are meaningful, and about the ramifications of these meanings. In other words, educators can integrate their knowledge of children, observations, reflections, and study of children's work and use this information to plan next steps. In this way, documentation becomes a planning tool for a rich and responsive curriculum.

## INVITATION TO EXPLORE

- Think about the children you are currently working with and their play explorations. What questions arise for you about this play? How can you pursue the answers to your questions? Choose one question to focus on, and keep notes or photographs that pertain to it. Can you assemble these data into a small documentation panel?

- Ask someone who is not associated with your children or classroom to take a look at your documentation. What does this person take away from the work? Is it what you intended?

- Where would you place yourself in the documentation progressions Wien described? What is the next step in your documentation journey? What kinds of supports do you need to move forward and deepen your documentation practices?

# Design and Photography

Whether we are aware of it or not, design affects every aspect of our daily lives. In subtle ways, design influences our everyday decisions, such as what kind of wrapping paper to buy for a special gift, the choices we make when setting up a home, the types of logos we are willing to wear on our clothing, and much more. Design is everywhere, and it either attracts or repels us.

Of course, one of the goals of pedagogical documentation is to entice viewers to explore the documented work further. We want parents and other adults to understand the learning we are attempting to make visible. We want them to read the text without becoming distracted, to easily find their way through the visual layout, and to use the photographs or traces of children's work to support their understanding of the documented event. Of course, it is also important that the children themselves be able to find their way through the visuals and be able to clearly see what they experienced and investigated during the project or moment.

To entice viewers, we need to understand some design basics. This is true for early childhood educators, teacher educators, and administrators alike. I am not a graphic designer, so to supply this information, I reached out to Annette Comeau, an early childhood educator in Halifax, Nova Scotia. Annette also holds a degree in art education and graphic design and is inspired by the practices of Reggio Emilia. She visited the Italian preschools in 2007, and here is what she has to say about the documentation that she saw there.

### Annette Comeau on Italian Documentation

When I looked at the documentation panels on display at the Reggio centers in Italy, I found it was important to remember that the work had passed through many hands. First, the teachers and pedagogistas had

(cont'd)

23

met to interpret and to understand the work of the children. (The term *pedagogista* refers to "a master teacher . . . who works with several schools and takes part in dialogue on subjects that range from projects to design, parent issues, teacher education, budget, children with special needs, and more" [Lewin-Benham 2011, 200].) Then, through discussion and analysis, they had distilled the work down to its essence, which was assembled into finished panels.

Of course, this kind of collaboration does not occur often in North America. So I turned my focus toward small displays created by the teachers and displayed at the children's level in the classrooms. These displays were obviously created by the teachers. I found them to be some of the most interesting pieces of documentation.

I saw carefully matted pictures, sculptures in recycled transparent boxes, and class books bound in interesting ways. The Reggio teachers did not write the children's names directly on the work but instead created typed name tags. Items were matted and hung carefully along with information about the work. I noticed individual folders containing children's art and larger folders for storing larger pieces. It was evident that the teachers took great care to follow the children's processes and to create an archive of their learning. Each center was equipped with computers, printers, and cameras to aid in this archiving process. However, it was clear that the teachers were not only creating memories for the children, but were also presenting the children's work back to them for further consideration and discovery.

I found all of this to be very exciting. I felt that these were the types of things that my colleagues and I could accomplish in our own classrooms if we were careful to treat the children's work with respect and to display it in an artful and thoughtful manner.

## APPLYING THESE IDEAS IN NORTH AMERICA

It is unusual in North America to have supports as wonderful as those Annette saw in Reggio Emilia. And we cannot simply transplant philosophies and approaches from other cultures into our own. They may inspire us, but we must reinvent them to fit within or supplement our own philosophies and cultures.

We can begin to do this simply but with goals in mind. Annette and I reflected on what initial goals might be in terms of both designing and assembling documentation. Here, in Annette's words, are some ideas to consider.

### Annette Comeau on Documentation Design and Assembly

To get your feet wet with documentation design, you might try documenting a small, interesting moment involving one or two children. For instance, begin by taking four or five photographs. Then, by reflecting upon these photos, try to describe the process in writing as well as giving this small moment a visual form. Documentation of a large project can involve much editing and thought before you even get to the visual presentation. This can be overwhelming. But by keeping your first documentation small, you can focus mainly on the presentation, the logistics, and the making of a documentation panel. You may feel more comfortable working with less material. Once you have succeeded with something small, you will gain the confidence to move on to a larger project.

### *Text Design*

Keep your text design simple—especially when you are working with the typeface in your document. People should notice the photographs and the children's work first, rather than a splashy (bold, underlined, stretched, outlined, or otherwise attention-grabbing) typeface. Type effects can be tempting, but too much play with the type in documentation interferes with the message, is distracting, and is visually tiring. I use a typeface called Futura, which is often available on computers as Century Gothic. It is a visually simple sans serif typeface. In addition, this typeface contains the "primary *a*," which is the type of lowercase *a* that children learn to print first. I feel that this is important when we are sharing documentation

with children. I also use specific sizes for titles and headings.
I do this for visual consistency when I am creating multiple documentation panels that are meant to be viewed together, or when I am creating the pages of a portfolio. I make the main points in a slightly larger font, for viewers who have only enough time to browse quickly. I put the fine details in a smaller font, for those who really want to read further.

### *Photographs*

Choose specific, consistent sizes of photographs. For instance, your small ones could always be two inches (five centimeters) wide, the larger

(cont'd)

ones always four inches (ten centimeters), and so on. Once again, this creates visual consistency over many documentation panels. The size of the photographs is also one way to indicate to the viewer how you would like them to consider the information that you are presenting. Viewers generally see larger images first. Therefore, you can use size to help you organize your information. It is helpful to have a key picture that catches the viewer's attention. Sometimes a large photograph presented in the right way can set the tone for the whole project. For instance, my coworker Jennifer took a wonderful, close-up, detailed photo of a snail, which we enlarged and put on the wall. It set the tone for our whole project and the documentation panels describing the project. Ask yourself, "What is the key moment or moments that really tell what happened? How can I show this?" When people view a wonderful photograph, they tend to say, "Wow, that's really neat! What's going on here?" and then they look at your documentation more closely. All documentation should allow the viewer to experience it on different levels—from a quick reading of the large titles and images to a careful consideration of the more detailed descriptions presented in smaller images and text. This type of organization is called a hierarchy of information.

### White Space

White space gives the viewer's eye somewhere to rest. This is why pictures are not all hung close together in art galleries. In documentation, leave margins between the text and the page edge, and space between photos and text. Remember that documentation is not scrapbooking. Decoration is not necessary. In fact, it detracts from the children's work. Let the children's work shine. You might use your word-processing software to justify blocks of text in order to create a "clean" effect.

### Big Projects

How do you handle a big project that spans several months? You're going to have to start out by looking at everything—all the notes you've jotted, photos you've taken, and traces of children's work you've saved. But remember that you can't include everything in the documentation, because it will be too cumbersome and daunting, and few people will take the time to read it. So you have to make some decisions. What do you want people to know about this project? One way to begin is to put away all your notes and pictures and just tell someone—perhaps a colleague—the story of what happened: "First we did this, we responded with that, and then the children did this." By simply telling the story, you are making a road map for yourself and creating simple signposts to follow. You can expand on these ideas later when you have a clear understanding of the whole project. Think about the signposts you mentioned when telling your story. You can hang information onto each one. What should go with these images and ideas? By the time you are ready to create a documentation panel, you will have distilled the project down to its essence.

### *Practical Tips for Assembling Documentation by Hand*

- When creating text for panels or when creating matted art, I use text boxes created in my word-processing program. The computer does the centering and makes everything straight for cutting and mounting. I can cut easily along the lines of the box in which the text is contained.

- When I cut, I use a utility knife called an X-Acto knife and a metal ruler. I use the ruler to hold my knife steady and to cut a straight line. I find that scissors aren't very accurate. It is difficult to cut a true straight line with scissors. A really good knife works better and with some practice is much faster. The knife must be sharp.

- A cutting mat with a grid is very useful. Its gridlines help me keep things square. The mat also grips the paper somewhat, which helps with neat, safe cutting.

- I use a right triangle and a long ruler to keep items straight and square to the edges of the board. A T-square is another option, but a triangle is helpful for placing things on an angle. I use light pencil marks for placement guidance.

Annette's design advice may seem like a daunting amount of information to consider, especially if you are new to documentation. But learning to create documentation is like any other new activity; it gets easier with practice. When our tools are organized and accessible and when we have practiced on small pieces, documentation becomes an enjoyable and engaging experience—a creative and thoughtful process that validates the work of both children and adults.

## PLANNING TIPS

- Think about the data (notes, photos, and work samples) that you have at hand. What format would best suit this information? Horizontal (landscape) or vertical (portrait) orientation? Should you place text to the side of the photographs or underneath them? Lay out your work without gluing at first, so you can consider the effect. Is it what you intended?

- As you begin to prepare the text, think about font size. To make a decision about font size, you need to know *where* you will be using the documentation. How close will the viewer be to the work? If viewers will be standing back (viewing a wall-mounted display, for example), then the text will need to be quite large and simple (sixteen to eighteen points minimum, and about thirty-six points for headings). A smaller font might be manageable for close-up viewing, such as in a logbook or portfolio.

- On what kind of surface will you mount the work? Foam board? Bristol board? Or will you be attaching the work and photos to a line with bulldog clips or clothespins? If you're mounting the work, think about the type of adhesive that would be most appropriate. Liquid glue tends to seep through paper, and excess glue causes wrinkling. Spray adhesive is very effective and allows for repositioning. It needs to be used in a well-ventilated space. Double-sided tape can be useful but is often needed in great quantities and can become expensive.

## A FEW THOUGHTS ABOUT PHOTOGRAPHY

Before we take photos of children to use within documentation, let's pause to think about what we are trying to achieve. We all have slightly different goals. Yet we also have one overall goal in common: we want people to understand the thinking, learning, and ideas behind the children's actions. The photographs we take should support that goal.

Sometimes, we take a special photo that captures a wonderful aha moment in a child's exploration. That one photograph almost says it all. It needs only a little text to complete the viewer's understanding.

In other instances, we need a whole series of photos in order to show how an investigation unfolded. And sometimes just three or four images can clearly illustrate a big investigation.

Reflection is a key part of the documentation process. When we carefully examine our images and discuss them with team members *before* placing them onto a documentation panel, we are forced not only to articulate what happened and how but also to think about which photographs best explain the child's process. Which images successfully carry the story forward in an understandable way? What questions arise for teachers while viewing these photographs, and what kind of inquiry will lead us to the answers to these questions?

## Photo Quality

Using digital devices and applications with which we can edit the photos we've taken makes it easier than ever to produce images that are clear and close-up and that capture the action in a busy classroom. The cameras on smartphones, for instance, are often able to compensate for such challenges as low light and fast action. A tablet may not take still photos as crisp as those from a digital camera but may capture beautiful video clips. And if we have digital single-lens reflex (DSLR) cameras on hand, then we can produce almost professional-quality photos.

The quality of photos is so important. Why? Let's remember that we are not photographing cute events or poses. We are trying to capture learning in action, the beauty of a child's artwork, the thinking, experimentation, and ideas behind children's inquiries, or an aha moment that is expressed—just for a second—on a child's face. Here are some examples. In taking these photographs, the photographer tried to zero in on the action within the event and the facial expressions that broadcast children's feelings or thinking.

A moment of discovery: S. finds a letter from her name. The children had been using magnetic letters on a metal board. S. experienced a moment of delight—clearly shown in this photograph—when she recognized an *a* as being a part of her name. Since most children at this time were focused on the first letters of their names, this was a significant event for her. She realized that words are made of several letters, all of them important.

Hands at work: Using string and wire to hold objects together was a new challenge for most of our children, yet one that they were very interested in taking on. Genevieve's concentration and care is evident in this photograph. The challenge was so engaging that rather than frustrating Genevieve, it produced determination.

Close-ups of hands in action are often important to include when projects or investigations include actions upon or with materials.

Inquiry in action: Access to magnifying glasses has resulted in children looking more closely at everything in their environment. This close observation is an important aspect of figuring out how things work. Everything from the natural world to the fine differences within printed words is important to the children these days, as they learn how to look and to see more closely.

This photo demonstrates how children are using this new tool. It appeared in our daily logbook, but it also facilitates teachers' thinking about how children see details in the world around them.

Archiving children's art: In the studio area of the classroom, we were working on building artwork over several days. For instance, we made watercolor backgrounds of the savannah and together thought about what else the children might want to add on top of their backgrounds, rather than considering their paintings finished. Some children chose to add animals, while others chose trees that seemed to be leaning in the wind. Slowing down during artwork resulted in more intentional paintings by most children.

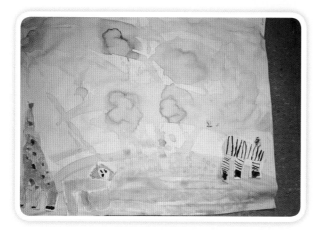

## Some Practical Tips

According to people who take professional photographs of children, we must pay attention to three main practical aspects of photography:

1. Lighting: While a good flash will compensate for an underlit room, there is nothing quite as beautiful as natural light, especially if it is illuminating the subject from a unique angle. Outdoors, of course, natural light is easy to come by. Yet outdoors, we must be careful that the children are not backlit, that is, positioned with sunlight behind them. Backlighting throws the children into shadow, obscuring the details of the children themselves.

2. Composition: While we certainly do not want posed photos for documentation purposes, we should try to eliminate background clutter, which may be distracting. Fortunately, most of us have some sort of editing tool on our computers, so that we can crop to our heart's content. With your cropping tool, you can often eliminate a messy shelf alongside a child, or a friend who is playing to the camera and distracting attention from the child or work that is really the focus of the image.

3. Distance: Get closer! Adults tend to make a common mistake when photographing children: we stand too far away. Perhaps we don't want to intrude on the children's play, or perhaps children tend to stop and pose if they notice us. Instead, we should use a telephoto lens or the zoom function on a smartphone. A photograph of a child in action is so much more effective

when taken at close range. We must also take care to get down to the children's level. Photographs of the tops of children's heads are of no use. What we really want to emphasize is their hands and their work. This photograph, for instance, is close enough to show that the child is learning to sew, and it captures the look of concentration on his face.

## A FINAL WORD: THE IMPORTANCE OF NAMING DOCUMENTATION

Titles matter. They give a clue as to what the reader is about to experience. And if titles are somewhat creative, they can be delightful, intriguing, thought provoking, and inviting. The tone of the title leads the reader into the work. For instance, instead of "Exploring Sand," use something like "The Fascination of Sand: Exploring Wet and Dry Materials." Or rather than "Our Community Partners," use "Reaching Out to the Community: Collaboration in Action."

Often, a quote from a child can provide a wonderful title. We just have to listen and consider: What is the core of this piece? How can it best be described? How can we illuminate the children's work?

## INVITATION TO EXPLORE

- Of the photographs within this chapter, which one speaks most clearly to you? What does it say? How does it convey this message?

- With a digital camera, take five photographs of the same play from different perspectives. (If you are a student teacher in an adult learning environment, photograph other students using loose parts—those collections of interesting bits and pieces that are open-ended and therefore can be used in many ways.) Reflect upon the photographs afterward. If you had to choose one photo for documentation purposes, which would it be, and why?

- Using your photos, lay out a documentation panel with text. Do not glue down your pieces, but try moving them around to see what effects different arrangements have on the whole.

- Consider a suitable title for your documentation piece. How does your title encapsulate what is happening within the panel?

# The Chocolate Project

When you're developing any skill, it's often helpful to reflect upon the work of others who've gone through the process before you. Through viewing several different types of documentation from varied settings, you are likely to find an example that speaks to you and inspires you. You will see over the next few chapters that there are many ways to approach pedagogical documentation. How you choose to document children's thinking, play, and learning will depend on your own experiences, your comfort level, the work you want to document and the questions that arise for you out of this work, the children themselves, and the time and supports that you have available.

In this chapter, we will examine a project that lasted several weeks in the junior primary classroom (composed of four- and five-year-olds) at Halifax Grammar School, where I was the primary coordinator as well as a classroom teacher. Through examining and reflecting on this long-term project, we will see which items teachers chose for large documentation panels, how they presented the items, and the text that was written to explain the work. We will also see which items teachers chose from this project for individual portfolios. Why did they use these items in these ways, and how did they make these decisions?

## FROM POTIONS TO CHOCOLATE

Let's begin this journey with a little background. The seventeen four- and five-year-old children and three staff in our junior primary classroom were sometimes joined by practicum students in their first or second year of study at the Nova Scotia College of Early Childhood Education. We were always delighted to welcome these students. They added enthusiasm and new ideas to our own thinking. And they helped us in another important way, too. When we are working on emergent curriculum with student teachers, we have a responsibility to articulate our thinking out loud; this is a great way to further our own development. While working with student teachers, we are in a heightened state of reflection. We know that we can't assume anything about what the students see and understand. We know we must make all our knowledge and thinking explicit for their sakes. Documentation helps us with the process of making the teachers' thinking—as well as the children's—visible to others.

The Chocolate Project did not begin with chocolate. It began with "potions." For two or three weeks, we had been observing the children's fascination with mixing anything that was available—soil and water, cornstarch, colors (with pipettes). They baked many kinds of materials, and they made playdough. Some mixtures fizzed, others created wonderful color swirls, and still others separated out into layers. The children called their mixtures potions, and their experimentation went on for weeks. If it was mixable, the children mixed it.

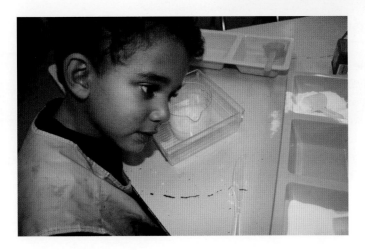

During this time, our student teacher Blair was also watching the children closely. One day she provided several spices as well as powders such as cocoa and mustard for the children to mix in small quantities. Blair wondered if the addition of scent to the children's potions would make a difference in the children's experimentation. Were they interested in *what* they were making? Or was this entirely about the mixing process?

Blair and I photographed and wrote constantly as the investigation unfolded. Following are several photos of what happened, with explanations. Later, you will see which photos we chose to use for documentation purposes and how we later put all of these together into a series of panels, along with a rationale for why and how we made these decisions.

These are the materials offered by Blair as an invitation during play. After guessing what each cup contained, the children then chose what to use and mixed their own potions. We took dozens of photographs like this one, accompanied by notes about the children's conversations as they worked.

The children returned to mixing cocoa over and over again. They constantly commented on the smell. At this time, Blair casually remarked that cocoa comes from trees. The children reacted with disbelief, telling us, "No, it comes from the store!" We teachers asked ourselves, "What can we offer as an exploration or invitation to expand the children's knowledge of where cocoa and chocolate come from?"

It proved to be impossible to have a hands-on experience with cacao pods, since the nearest place they grow is in Mexico, and we could not find an importer who had the whole pod. However, we did find a child-narrated video set within the rain forest of Costa Rica that explained cocoa and chocolate production, with a young child demonstrat-

ing the whole process. Also, after a long search, we were able to find a few cacao beans in a nearby coffee- and chocolate-roasting facility and some cacao nibs (which

come from the inside of the bean) in the organic section of a grocery store. The children drew these items, smelled them, and played with them in the dramatic play area. Upon reflection, we realized that the children still did not associate these items with chocolate, even though many books had been provided for their research and we had engaged in lots of discussions. They needed further experiences in order to make the connection.

Since the children knew from the video that cacao nibs must be crushed before they can be used, we provided mortars and pestles for them to try crushing nibs in the dramatic play area. They spent days working on this. It was difficult work, but the children were motivated, since they wanted to bake with the resulting powder. We heard such comments as "This is hard work!" and "My arm is aching!" yet no one wanted to give up. For teachers, this is a testament to the hard work that children are willing to do when they are intrigued with a process.

During this time, we constantly reviewed what had happened through photography that we shared with the children. At one morning meeting, the children put the photos of their investigation into chronological order. Since we had no cacao pod, we used a football as a stand-in because it was the same shape as a cacao pod—an idea that came from the children.

Gradually, the children began referring to the dramatic play area as their chocolate factory. The teachers wondered how the children could make a stand-alone chocolate factory, and if they were interested in such a challenge. We offered an invitation consisting of an assortment of technical odds and ends, general loose parts, and a supporting framework on which to build. Some children took up this invitation with great enthusiasm and worked on this structure for several days.

A problem occurred when the children tried to send nibs down the chute into the "grinding part." Everything bounced back out of the "catching container"! After some experimentation, two girls working together figured out that a piece of netting could prevent the nibs from bouncing back out of the container. They took a whole morning playtime to figure this out, and they did it completely independently.

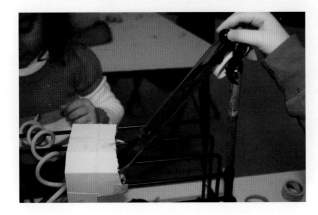 

The availability of a piece of netting on the studio shelves demonstrated the value of odds and ends and loose parts as a support for children's experimentation, problem solving, and learning.

Construction of the chocolate factory continued for two weeks. As the children devised different "machinery," we encouraged them to explain how the machinery worked and to draw the process of how the beans became chocolate going through the machine. We added small labels that the children dictated, such as "the crushing part" or the "pouring part." This work demonstrated the children's theories—both what they had understood from the books we had read and their viewing of the video. They were very clear, based on their own experiences crushing nibs, that the chocolate factory had to have a crushing part.

The children shared their completed chocolate factory with the school community by placing it on a small table outside our classroom. Families, older students, and other teachers stopped by to look. A frequent comment from older children was "How come we didn't get to do this when *we* were in junior primary?"

## DECIDING WHAT TO DOCUMENT

From the hundred or so photographs that we took during this project, we naturally had to make some choices about which ones we would use in our documentation. Here are some considerations that we kept in mind while making these choices:

- Which photographs show best how the project developed over time?

- What were the teachers' reflections and questions, and how can these be made visible through photography and text?

- Which photos demonstrate the children's thinking, ideas, and problem solving?

- How much wall space do we have available?

- For whom is this documentation intended? The children? Families? Other teachers? All of these? What difference does audience make in regard to our photo choices?

- What about the quality of the photographs? Are the ones under consideration sharp enough? Close enough? Do they really show what we want to show?

- How much room do we have available for text?

- Do we have permission from families to use the photographs we've chosen?

The number of panels in our documentation was limited by wall space—a common challenge in early childhood classrooms. We reminded ourselves that the chocolate factory itself was a piece of documentation, as were the photos we'd chosen for the children's portfolios. We realized that we could eliminate these photos as well as those meant to show the chocolate factory's construction from the documentation panels.

Our classroom had only a few small wall spaces available at this time, due to the placement of windows, doors, cubbies, and storage units. Since these wall spaces were already in use for other recent documentation, our new panels had to be placed in the hallway outside the classroom on a fairly small bulletin board. Although this location offered exposure to the whole school community, it limited our ability to show the big picture. So we focused on the core "landmarks" of the project. Here are the final photo choices we made for the documentation panels, with explanations.

These photographs were chosen for their close-up views of the details of mixing, which is where the project

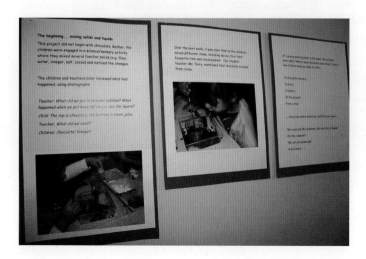

began. The text explains this beginning phase to set a context for how the work evolved. It is clear in one of the photographs that the children think cocoa is the most interesting powder. We mounted the photographs and text on brown construction paper, which provides a frame for the documentation, and we hung them in a simple horizontal line for easy viewing by the reader. The text is in sixteen-point Comic Sans, one of the few typefaces that uses the primary *a*. (We use Comic Sans often, for the benefit of the young children in our classroom who are just beginning to read.)

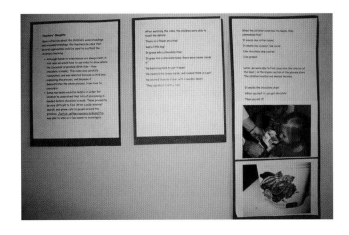

In this documentation text, we describe the puzzle of how to scaffold the children's learning about chocolate. Although this panel may seem wordy, it is as brief as we could make it while enabling the reader to understand the teachers' challenges in terms of what to do next. The text mentions community support for our next steps (the wide hunt for real cacao beans) and the age-appropriate video. We included this information to make visible the teachers' commitment and effort. The activities are intentional, carefully thought through, and as child-centered as we could make them.

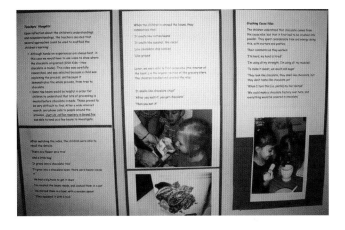

The discovery of real cacao nibs moved our project forward significantly, so the introduction of this material seemed important to document. The children used the cacao nibs in many ways, and the photographs chosen for documentation give a little taste of their experiences. The text explains further, and it links the activities and the children's words as they worked.

Each day throughout the project, the children and teachers reviewed the previous day's work by examining photos, either printed on paper or enlarged on a laptop. In this way, the children were able to remember their work and expand on their ideas. Teachers had the opportunity to ask further questions to either clarify what the children were saying or help the children expand

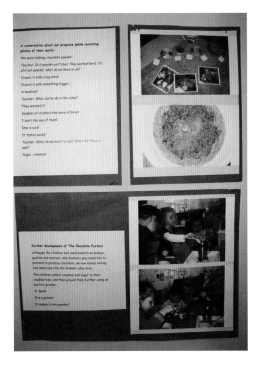

their thinking. One photograph on this panel shows the children's version of how the project had evolved so far; they put the photos in order and numbered them. (Note that the children numbered from right to left instead of left to right.) The next photograph is an important one. It moves the project from one phase (mixing, grinding, and baking with cacao nibs) to the next (construction of the chocolate factory). With limited space available, this seemed like a good place to pause. We displayed the next set of documentation pieces separately from the rest, as well as in individual children's portfolios.

We mounted the following two photographs and the next two separately from the preceding panels, with a description of what the children were trying to do (send nibs down the chute into a receptacle) and the ensuing problems (the nibs bounced out of the receptacle and onto the floor), as well as the solution (netting), which took considerable time and effort to reach. We chose to make a separate story of this episode due to the considerable efforts of two girls who solved the problem collaboratively. We also placed these photographs in their individual portfolios, along with a description of the trial and error that took place. When it was time to meet with families later in the year, we pointed to this episode as an example of cooperation, problem solving, and creative thinking.

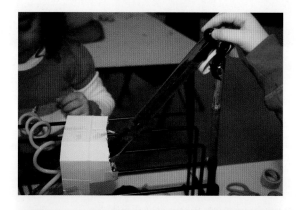

We documented another small episode separately, too. We made this decision because the main story was already complete. The children knew that we would eventually have to return the cacao beans we had borrowed from Just Us! Café in Wolfville, Nova Scotia. They were part of a display in the company's chocolate-production area, and Frank, our contact there, had generously offered to mail them to us to use for a short time. But the children were enjoying using the beans as a dramatic play prop. How could we preserve their play experiences when the beans went back home?

Since the children had originally enjoyed mixing so much, we offered them a chance to do more mixing by making modeling dough and then forming it into the shape of cacao beans for their own use during play. The children took up this invitation enthusiastically, and we photographed and commented on it in writing.

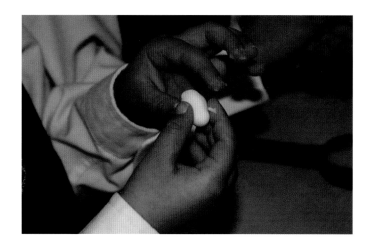

We shared the adjoining photograph, along with an explanation, in the logbook that sits outside our classroom. This book offers shorter pieces of documentation for families to read quickly when they pick up their children at the end of the day. Since they are usually in a hurry at this time of day, the logbook offers a starting point for conversations on the way home. This is a beloved part of the parents' and children's days—to look through the logbook, see one or two samples of things that happened that day, and chat with their children about the latest investigation. Although these pieces are not as reflective in tone as a fuller piece of documentation, they are still important for the following reasons:

- New logbook entries appear daily, offering a continuous flow of information to families and helping them keep up with changing events from day to day.

- They provide for constant communication between teachers, children, and families. The children enthusiastically explain the photos to their families.

- Older children, including alumni from our classroom, love to glance at the book while passing by, thereby keeping us in touch with the rest of the school.

- Small moments or shorter-term explorations are easy to represent in this format.

Once the children had drawn and modeled the beans, they were packaged up, ready to be mailed to the roastery. But we did not know the address. What should we do? These four-year-olds had a simple solution: "Just Google it!" And so we did. They helped me search online for the roastery, dictate a letter of thanks to Frank, and mail the package.

As well as being a part of the overall story, we felt that this work demonstrated children's ideas about how to communicate in writing, where to get information, and how we use conventional ("snail") mail. We also discussed the importance of thanking community partners for their contribution to our investigation. This vignette was of great interest to families since the children talked about Frank (our contact) at home, even though they had never met him.

Our chocolate factory project shows how teachers can document and share a long-term investigation in many different ways. But what about shorter investigations or small yet special moments? These occur constantly in a richly provisioned environment. In the next chapter, we will take a look at several such investigations and moments and how the teachers documented them.

## INVITATION TO EXPLORE

- After reading the account of the two girls who solved the problem of beans bouncing away, imagine making a documentation piece about just this event. What would the title be? How does your title encapsulate the challenge and draw people in to read further?

- Here are two photographs from this project, both showing the grinding of cacao nibs with mortars and pestles. If you had to choose one to demonstrate the effort involved in grinding, which one would it be, and why?

# 4

# Documenting Extraordinary Moments and Short Explorations

## THOSE SPECIAL MOMENTS

If you have worked in early childhood education for any length of time, you know that special moments occur throughout the day, every day, with young children. What do these moments look like? Here are some examples from my own experiences as well as from those of colleagues around North America:

- A toddler demonstrates making a connection between an illustration in a book and a real-life object by placing the object next to the illustration and showing it to you.

- After hearing an account of a distressed bird flying into a windowpane, a preschool child quietly goes off to construct tall buildings with windows in the block area.

- A child who is emerging into literacy begins to make written signs to share information with other children.

In addition to extraordinary moments, early childhood educators also regularly see short-term investigations and experiences. Here are a few examples:

- A classroom pet dies, and over a two-day period, a group of children creates a grave in the outdoor play space and buries the pet.

- Over a period of one week, two boys invent a game around the difficult task of making a ball land and stay on a narrow ledge.

- A sudden explosion of experimental print occurs in the classroom, with children using many strategies to write words or represent written language in other ways.

- The addition of a stuffed real owl to the classroom creates a flurry of interest in birds, and a short investigation emerges.

- A royal wedding generates huge interest from the girls in the classroom, and it gradually draws in the boys.

When the investigation or experience is short, then teachers can document it in a small, brief way. Whether mounted on a quarter-sheet of Bristol board or on heavy paper, documentation for special moments and short explorations can be quickly and simply produced. However, such documentation should still address the meaning behind the moments with carefully considered photography and text. And simple moments may still generate complex questions for teachers to pursue. Following are some examples of documentation of extraordinary moments and short explorations. Each example presents the documentation first, followed by text explaining how the documentation came about and/or how the piece was eventually used.

*Poor Bird*

At morning meeting today, we read a story about a bird that flew into a high-rise window and fell to the ground, stunned. The children were greatly concerned about this idea, and we discussed at some length how and why birds sometimes do this. During the following play period, we noticed a child building with interlocking cubes and then adding window tiles to her building. A teacher quietly placed the book next to the child. She glanced at the illustrations from time to time,

(cont'd)

eventually retelling the story aloud in her own words. The next day, other children joined in this building activity. They appeared to be confused about whether the story had contained windows or mirrors, so we offered mirrors on which to build, which helped clarify the difference between windows and mirrors. We wonder if this investigation of building was an expression of sympathy for the bird, and we wonder how we can pursue this question further.

Due to the children's overall interest in birds, and in particular the fallen bird, we took this piece of documentation back to the children at our morning meeting for further discussion. The discussion seemed to help the children reflect on what had happened to the bird in the story and why it happened. The bird survived, and they seemed relieved by that. "It'll be okay. It was just knocked out for a bit," they said. In addition, we were able to clarify that sometimes a transparent window can reflect like a mirror. The teachers began to think about ways for children to experiment with this concept at the science table and at our light table. In this way, the birds-and-buildings exploration generated a short investigation of light and reflection.

### A Moment of Friendship

This friendly moment occurred in the writing area, as children experimented with print. Since it is early in the semester, we are watching for signs of connections between children as they form new relationships. In this case, printing alongside each other provided a shared experience. Both children have an *S* in their name, and they discovered this while watching each other print their names. This moment demonstrates for us the power of shared experiences—the delight in discovering something with a partner, finding a connection, and being together in that moment. We will continue to search for ways for children to work together.

We printed two copies of this documentation and placed one in each child's portfolio. We also e-mailed it to one child's mother, who was comforted to see her daughter interacting with other children after a shy and tentative beginning at school.

### An Invented Game

A. and S. were drawn to each other, despite some language challenges that occasionally created misunderstandings. On this morning, S. was playing with a ball against a wall, when to his surprise, it suddenly became stuck on a narrow ledge. A. thought that this was fascinating, and the two boys spent the whole of their outdoor time over several days collaborating in trying to make this happen again and again—often succeeding! This game needed no spoken language, only imagination and persistence; we might call it the language of play.

At our morning meeting, we shared this documentation with all the children, who later joined in with this game during outdoor time. A. and S. were visibly pleased and proud of having made up such an intriguing game. We placed this documentation piece in each child's portfolio and in the daily log, where the boys' parents saw it and subsequently heard their children's explanations.

### Visions of a Stormy Day

After reading *The Rainy Day* by Anna Milbourne and Sarah Gill on a particularly stormy day in Nova Scotia, several children went to the easel during playtime and represented their ideas of a stormy day. This response was quite spontaneous, which led us to think about the many ways in which children absorb knowledge about their world and then represent their understanding through many "languages." The children's paintings give varied representations of the concept of a storm. In the photo on the top left, the darkness of the whole is striking. The child needed to mix black and white in several ways to get this effect. The other photos demonstrate another child's thinking about how a storm develops; the child added gray raindrops to the clouds and a sprinkling of dripping paint to represent rain falling onto the ground. We see connected understandings of this event demonstrated in two completely different ways. These ten minutes at the easel remind us to watch carefully, since children often show us their understandings of the world around them without using words.

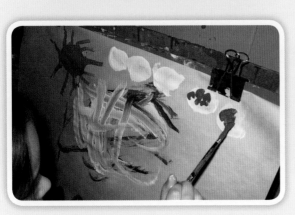

We mounted these paintings onto larger paper that served as a frame. We discussed them at our morning meeting, and then we hung them in the studio area at the children's eye level. Easel watching has since become an important form of observation for our team, as paintings produced there often represent children's thoughts about what they have recently seen or heard.

*A Spatial Problem*

The teachers placed a giant sunflower next to the easel, with no comment, as a provocation. Children had recently begun to create representational drawings and paintings, and we wondered how they would react to this enormous flower. M. immediately came over and began to paint. Since the flower was to his right, he began painting on that side of his paper, but he quickly ran out of space as he tried to paint the curve of the huge flower's stem. He paused and stared at his paper for some time, then looked around the room for a teacher. He explained the problem: "There's no more room!" The teacher responded, "Well, what could we do?" M. soon came up with the idea of taping more paper to the right side of the existing sheet. The teacher helped with this, and M. continued painting happily.

We shared this painting with the children at our morning meeting, along with paintings by other children, as a way of engaging in collaborative problem solving. What do we do when our paper is too small? What is just the right size for what we want to paint? Our small studio space eventually displayed a whole gallery of sunflower paintings.

## Investigating Birds

This investigation was short-lived (about two weeks) but quite intense in terms of the children's representations. It began when the children noticed birds coming to the feeder outside our classroom windows. We wondered together how we could

D. meets the owl for the first time. Its feathers seem to invite touching. All the children eventually noticed the intricate pattern on the feathers. Their prior knowledge became evident, since the children understood that this pattern was part of the owl's camouflage. We offered many ways for children to make representations of the bird: paint, clay, pencil, and so on.

The children's first paintings of the owl. We noticed that these paintings all follow the same schema, or way to paint an owl, rather than representing what the owl actually looks like. We therefore decided to offer different drawing materials, beginning with fine black markers.

The children's later drawings of the owl, as we examined it more closely (including with a magnifying glass). These drawings show much more intricate detail. We noticed that the children slowed down considerably when making these drawings. This reminded us of how powerfully the drawing tools affect how and what children draw.

Other media for representing birds included modeling clay. It is interesting to see that the use of modeling clay results in a two-dimensional bird with feathers radiating from a central space but no defined body. What meaning can we make of this? Are the wings the most important aspect of the bird for the child?

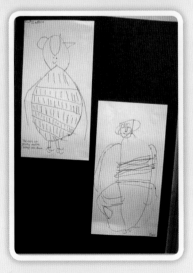

help the birds through the harsh winter. After creating many kinds of bird feeders, the children began talking of what they knew about birds in general. We supported this interest by providing many kinds of experiences, but the addition of a stuffed real owl as a provocation really moved the investigation to another level. Here is a sampling of our quick and simple documentation around this investigation.

We placed this documentation in our logbook daily. We also placed it on walls for the children to comment on. As you see on the previous page, we placed the owl paintings on an unused chalkboard with a brief note from a teacher, which simply states what happened first: "There is an owl in our classroom!" The children thought this comment was quite funny and often repeated the phrase.

## The Hundred Steps Meadow

The following documentation was created by Sandra Floyd, an educator at Epiphany Early Learning Preschool in Seattle, Washington.

*October 3, 2012*

Today we took a walking field trip over to the meadow. We had made regular trips this last summer to this special place, but not since the beginning of the school year. Last week I brought it up again, and because the weather has been so nice, we all decided it would be a good place to revisit. We would love to make this place a regular part of our classroom life, visiting each week regardless of weather, and fold this piece of land into our curriculum.

What I think is so amazing about this place is that it holds almost every aspect of our *image of the child*. You may remember that at our new parent orientation night, we opened with an activity that got at this concept. Each parent told a story about a special childhood memory, and then we all talked about why it resonated with him or her. A lot of the answers had the same themes as how we here at Epiphany hold our image of children and how we think children learn best: risk taking, a sense of being unsupervised, returning to the same place, being free, mastering a game or toy, being independent, feeling strong, or feeling competent. We hold the belief that children learn through self-initiated play and discovery.

At the meadow there are opportunities at every turn for the kids to play hard and strong. The wide-open space allows them to run fast for a good stretch. They can stop in the middle of a wide-open space or plunge into the trees and hide. I love how they will run so far and fast that I can't hear their conversation. This is a great way to have the feeling of being unsupervised (while being supervised) and feeling free and trusted to run out of earshot of your teachers.

Other ways the kids are playing hard and strong are on the big hills and with the sticks. We have sticks on our play yard, but sticks you find in the woods are different; they simply are better. At first the teachers were unsure if this hard full-body play should be accompanied by sticks, but we felt that we had to let go of that fear. Sticks are as much a part of the play and landscape as the grass and leaves. I watched S. and T. play a game that could only have been played in a park. T. was up in the tree looking down through a crack; S. was at the base of the tree holding up a stick for T. to hold. T. was trying to pull S. up to him, and then S. would have a turn trying to pull T. down. This was a great way to strengthen not only their friendship, but also their arms! They were able to play this for quite some time before T. invited S. up to his perch to "look for bad guys." This is a good example of how we view children's competencies, and this view can either enhance or limit their experiences.

(cont'd)

The hills at this park are another way for the kids to take risks and for us teachers to support this risk taking. One of the two hills is just steep enough that the kids pause in the middle of climbing and change their climbing strategy. Most try to run or walk straight up and then find that it is too steep for that and climb up the rest of the way using both hands and feet. The tricky part is going down. The majority of the kids now know to either slide all the way down on their bottoms or get down halfway and then, when the coast is clear, stand up and run like the wind down the rest of the hill. Every once in a while their legs wouldn't be able to keep up and they would fall hard at the bottom, but it has never been too hard that they didn't get up and do it again. The older kids are usually the ones to make this leap. The younger ones watch the older kids while scooting down inch by inch. I love how a simple hill can create such dare-devil behavior! For the smaller kids, going up is just as risky as going down. H. and L. took a couple of turns trying the big hill before they found a gentler slope and kept their

play there. Both girls would climb as far as they could on their feet and then drop to their knees to finish the climb crawling. Then they would stand up with big smiles and talk about how they would run down before each descent. It reminded me of the many times I have stood on the top of the slope with my snowboard trying to get up the courage to go back down.

I am excited to see how this park will transform, and therefore transform our games, when the rain finally starts. I can imagine the hill becoming a great mudslide, and the low trees that are dark and spooky now will

become great shelters for games. I would also imagine that the wide-open meadow will be used less and the majority of games will retreat into the woods. The games will take on the flavor of the seasons; they will turn inward and be more about home and coziness.

We hope to return to this part of the neighborhood once a week to form a relationship with this park. We want to extend our classroom into the outdoor environment. We would love to put on our rain gear, or heavy jackets and mittens, or our shorts and sunscreen and learn and play while the seasons change. I would love to know what you think about us kids and teachers taking this on as part of our curriculum. What can you imagine for us as we play and learn throughout this year in an outdoor classroom?

Sandra's thoughtful documentation illustrates for parents not only what has happened, but also her own thoughts about the events, as well as her hopes for the future.

## DOCUMENTING WITH CHILDREN

One wonderful aspect of this briefer form of documentation is that you can prepare it on the spot—in the classroom, during playtime or small-group time, with some of the children present. As you sit with them and put photographs together with text, verbal children can offer much information about their thinking and about how they engaged in the exploration. On occasion, if the information is particularly rich, you might use only such transcribed conversations to support the photographs. At other times, you might embed some words from the children in the account of the teachers' thinking about the experience.

Nonverbal children too will be highly intrigued to see themselves on your computer screen or in a printed photograph. In these cases, a teacher might choose to describe in the text the child's facial expressions, body language, or vocalizations, and then try to interpret the child's responses to the photographs.

What do children gain from documenting with you? First, this process empowers them. It gives them a say in how their work is described and how it appears to others. Perhaps there is one photograph that they prefer over another, or a drawing that they are particularly proud of. They can tell you whether they are happy with your description of what happened—whether you have it right from their point of view.

Second, when children see the serious attention that you give to the process of sharing their work and their thinking with others, they understand that you validate that work and thinking. All documentation has this effect, but often it is produced by teachers in isolation. One-on-one or small-group documentation created *with* the children, by contrast, highlights the process and leads to more interaction between children and teachers about the work.

Third, while collaborating with you in decision making, children learn to articulate ideas in a way that others can understand. When we read their words back to them, preschool children may understand that the description is not clear or isn't quite what they wanted to say. Describing for someone outside their familiar circle is a different process for most children than describing for their families or teacher. Children must make their thinking more explicit, because the unknown reader has no background context to draw on. Teachers can support this type of language learning by asking questions such as "Do you think (Mom/Dad/other kids/other teachers) will know what you mean?" or "The big kids/younger kids in our school don't know we are doing this project; what should we tell them so they understand?"

## Children as Photographers

Placing a camera in the hands of a child (even a toddler) gives us the opportunity to see their environment through their eyes. Digital cameras allow us to make this happen easily. They are quite sturdy and use simple point-and-shoot technology. Children can take dozens of photographs, because we can delete many if necessary.

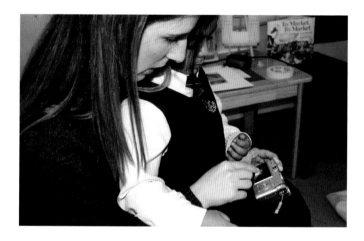

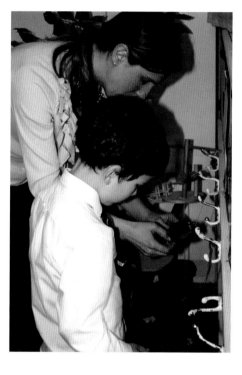

As children document what is important or interesting to them, we have a window into how they view the world. We can use these photographs for further conversations, both with the children and among teachers as part of the reflective process.

A teacher talks with a four-year-old about his photography: "Tell me about this photo." "This looks interesting; tell me more!" "What made you want a picture of this?" "What can we say about this photo to the other kids?" "Do we need more photos of this? What shall we do with them?"

## Children's Journals

I use the term *journal* loosely. In our classroom, each child had a small notebook for experimental print and for dictating to teachers. You can use such a journal, like a diary, to track what children are thinking about over long periods of time. For instance, if you store journals in a writing center on an accessible shelf, children

will use them for experimenting with print, making symbols, or dictating stories or memories. From time to time, they may wish to draw or talk about project work, ideas relating to how things work in their world, what is going on in their lives, and so on. No matter how small or tentative, these experimental print samples or drawings are all valuable traces of a child's prior knowledge, thinking, and experiences. Sometimes these experiences relate to what has been happening at home and are therefore a connection to families. They are documentation for us to reflect on.

It is clear that we have many opportunities every day to document small, extraordinary moments of learning and short-term investigations. To notice these moments requires vigilance. We must be willing to slow down in order to see what is unfolding before our eyes. This means having a system for jotting notes so that we don't forget the details, collaborating with team members, and assuming the mindset of a detective as we try to find out what specific moments mean to children. As my colleague Bobbi-Lynn Keating, executive director of Peter Green Hall Children's Centre, so aptly says, "We can snorkel—seeing what's close to the surface—or we can scuba dive and see more deeply."

## INVITATION TO EXPLORE

- Select a small moment of play that you have noticed recently. Describe it to a colleague or a fellow student teacher and discuss what may lie beneath the surface. What are the possibilities? What would you write as a piece of documentation about this moment?

- Try documenting *with* a child. Choose a couple of candid photos of the child at play and invite the child to tell you what was happening. Write down what the child says as the child says it, verbatim. It is important to respect and write down the child's own words. Assemble the transcript and the photos together on a page of documentation, and read it back to the child. What is the child's response?

# 5

# Connecting with Families through Documentation

Those of us who work with young children know how much thinking, effort, creativity, and intentionality we bring to our work. Although we are not often well compensated in the material sense, we find other wonderful rewards in our work. Feedback and engagement from the children's families can be encouraging and validating for us. How does pedagogical documentation support educators' efforts to build relationships with families? How does it promote families' understanding of what is happening in their children's classroom? How does it help them understand why we do the things we do? How does it bring parents into the life of the classroom?

Ann Lewin-Benham suggests in her book *Twelve Best Practices for Early Childhood Education* (2011) that documentation is a "magnet for parents." However, she also acknowledges the difficulty of involving parents in classroom life:

> It is not easy to involve parents in a school's daily life. Many parents do not have time. Some believe that they have no place in the school. Others are intimidated by what they perceive as teachers' superior education and knowledge. . . . There are as many barriers to families becoming involved as there are families. (Lewin-Benham 2011)

Lewin-Benham goes on to describe the powerful ways in which documentation drew in the families at the Model Early Learning Center (MELC) in Washington, DC, where she was director. Then she comments, "Without living through it, I am not sure I would have believed that documentation would be the impetus to involve parents in the daily life of the MELC" (39).

In my own practice, I experienced similar positive responses from families at Halifax Grammar School. These families had the opportunity to read documentation panels about long- and short-term investigations; view our logbook, which contained small daily events; and read their children's portfolios, which were more personalized. We asked them, "How did documentation further your understanding of how your child was learning, of how the program supported your child's thinking, or of how your child's ideas were developed into projects?"

Here is an example of a parent response:

> I found that documentation was very helpful for parents. It allowed us to know what the children were doing and gave lots of opportunities for discussion at home. My children would often reply to the question "How was school today?" with "Awesome!" but then not recount anything they had done. We had to prompt them with more questions, like "Did you do French today?" With the logbook, we could ask specifically about the activities we had seen there. I also thought that the documentation was very valuable because it allowed people who aren't early childhood education professionals to understand the inspiration and foundation behind each activity. This gave me confidence that my children's teachers knew exactly how best to teach them, using their interests as the basis for investigations. Finally, when parent-teacher interviews happened, it was great to see my children's work and to hear the teachers' thoughts on it.

When we make visible the children's ideas, understandings, misunderstandings, theories about how the world works, and active investigations, we are more likely to generate curiosity and engagement from their families. This chapter will discuss how early childhood settings can communicate with families about their children's work through various forms of documentation.

## INDIVIDUAL PORTFOLIOS

Naturally, family members want to read about and see their own children in action during play and investigations, want to witness their children's unfolding developmental stages, and want to examine work samples from their children. Individual portfolios perform all these functions, in addition to giving teachers a wealth of information for assessment purposes. Portfolios differ from setting to setting. They can contain any or all of the following:

- Photographs of the child in action, whether engaging in play, investigating materials, or taking part in activities. Written explanations should accompany these photos, explaining the context and significance of the events pictured.

When playing with an old (nonworking) laptop, L. provided his own screen image by drawing a maze and then placing it upon the blank screen. Later, he and M. created a game, drawing on several pages and then switching from page to page to enable the game to progress from one stage to another. We were excited to see such ingenuity and ability to transfer knowledge from one context to another.

- Traces of developmental milestones

H. created a message for other children using unconventional spelling. Her message reads, "Put your Lego on the overhead projector." This functional use of print demonstrates intentionality and a willingness to take a risk with writing. It also demonstrates H's desire to share her learning; she really wanted other children to experience the making of Lego shadows!

- Photographs or written descriptions of the child's social interactions

For several days, during play, children acted out going on a train journey. Most of them had never ridden on a real train, yet their prior knowledge—often from books—was impressive. With one child (always the same girl) as the station manager, the train was loaded with passengers, who had to have tickets. Provisions were found (including food for animals, who were taken along in cages), and even passports were developed.

We noticed much scaffolding between peers: one child explaining that passports were needed because they were leaving the country, another knowing that a whistle must blow before the train could leave. This play was rich, complex, and built on itself as the days went by. Teachers were clearly able to see leaders and willing followers and a steady building of knowledge.

In this case, photographs and text were placed in the station manager's portfolio as an example of her leadership abilities.

- Transcripts of conversations with the child. These conversational topics may include ideas, experiences, plans, or reflections on classroom events.

- Samples of the child's drawings, paintings, photographs of models or constructions, and so on. Such samples are traces of the child's classroom life and learning-in-action. Choose these samples carefully to avoid overcrowding the portfolio. Ask yourself, "Why am I including this?" or, "What is significant about this?" You can involve children in deciding what goes into their portfolios. If you keep portfolios in an accessible location and make them available to children for perusal, they will look at them often. Through frequent exposure to and conversations about their work, children learn that not everything goes into a portfolio—only items that are important to keep and share.

S. transfers her 3-D model of a bird into a 2-D format. This exploration of representation in different ways may open up further opportunities for S. to see her work and her thinking from several perspectives.

M. tries a new method (for him) of making marks. Since M. is not particularly fond of painting, this use of tools allowed him to explore paint effects in a different way.

After a discussion about quilts, this child constructed a design from odd fabric pieces, an activity that was the beginning of a larger exploration of quilts.

- Photographs and samples of project work. You can write one description of a project, with background information for context, and duplicate it for use in the portfolios of all the children who were involved in the project. Then you can write a more personalized comment for each child, commenting on the child's role within the project.

D. was fascinated by a skeleton puzzle provided as an invitation in the reading area. After assembling the puzzle, he independently found a nonfiction book to use as a reference for drawing a skeleton of his own. Then, he placed his drawing next to the puzzle skeleton and seemed to be deep in thought. Approaching a teacher, he showed her his drawing and stated, "I like mine better." D. is able to represent his world in many ways.

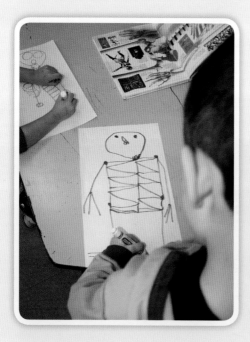

## LOGBOOKS

Like portfolios, logbooks differ from setting to setting. In most cases, however, log-books give a brief daily glimpse into classroom life by showing selected unrelated moments. In addition, a documented daily series of connected moments can provide an overview of a project's development. Daily pages may look like this:

October 1<sup>st</sup>

When a new globe with 3-D effects was introduced to the children at morning meeting, it was an opportunity for them to think about yesterday's idea that the Earth is 'bumpy' rather than smooth. It was hard to actually see the bumps (i.e. mountain ranges) even with a magnifying glass, but a gentle touch with fingers enabled the children to feel the raised areas.

Or in the case of connected events, daily pages may look like this:

The movement of paint: Over several days, the children have experimented with ways to move paint. They have used their hands and various tools, have moved the paper itself, and have also painted to music. These experiences have widened their view of what media may be able to do, as well as how to combine media. These experiences were first offered as an invitation after teachers noted a limited use of painting techniques. The invitation then took on a life of its own—or

(cont'd)

a life that was generated by children—as they realized that they preferred some techniques over others. The loose parts and wide range of tools in the studio will, we predict, lead to more experimentation and widen the children's language of art.

## WEEKLY NOTES

Many early childhood education settings send home weekly notes that give an overview of what has happened in the classroom. These notes may be in hard copy or electronic format, depending on families' circumstances and preferences. Either way, you can attach small pieces of documentation to these weekly notes, along with the usual news and reminders for families. As you assemble these pieces, keep in mind that they must fit within your usual format.

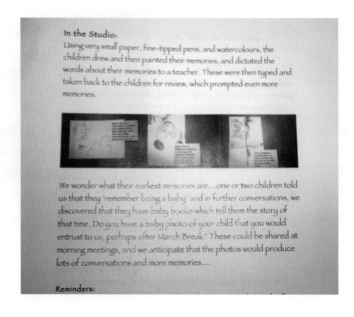

## BOOKLETS TO TAKE HOME

Some documentation lends itself well to being shared in booklet form. Booklets are very accessible and attractive to young children in the classroom, and they are also easy to send home to families. Since many parents and caregivers already read to their children at bedtime, booklets provide an opportunity to read the story of a project or event together, with the child doing most of the "reading." You can circulate booklets like these among all the parents over time.

## VIDEO

You can use video as a form of documentation for any audience at any time, but it is particularly useful for sharing projects involving music, movement, or a great deal of physical action such as climbing, setting play materials in motion, or building large structures outdoors. For investigations like these, video can give a sense of the kinesthetic learning that's involved, the grace and balance that's developing, the interpretations of music that are underway, and so on. If you are technically adept, you can do voice-overs for your videos. But voice-overs are not usually necessary. In most cases, if well filmed, the children's actions speak for themselves.

Annette Comeau, whom we met in a previous chapter, offers the example of a ballet project that unfolded in her toddler classroom:

> We felt that video, shared during a parent meeting, was the most suitable format for documentation of this topic. And, looking at the documentation again, we are thinking about hanging photographs from something that moves . . . one of those clothespin carousel things . . . which would move and give a sense of the project.

If you enjoy experimenting with still photographs, you can create movement effects by changing shutter speed. This technique is demonstrated in the photograph below, contributed by photographer Hannah Minzloff, who visited our classroom and shared her expertise during our photography project.

## THE UNEXPECTED ATTRACTS ATTENTION

As humans, we are often attracted to the unexpected—novel approaches to familiar routines, unusual ways of seeing things, and new ways of thinking about things. We are also attracted to beauty, such as the natural beauty of nature, the work of accomplished artists, and the uninhibited beauty of children's work.

When we plan documentation to attract attention to what children are doing and to invite people to make meaning of these events, we must also consider how the documentation will draw people in. In chapter 2, we explored design features and why they are important. When the documentation is complete, how will we use creative display—perhaps in unexpected places or in unusual ways—to attract the attention of our intended audience?

Perhaps you have a bulletin board or a wall near where children hang their belongings or where parents sign in and sign out their children. It is logical to use this space for documentation display. But if your documentation is always in the same place or hung in the same way, busy families may pass by without a glance. How can we do things a little differently to inspire curiosity? Here are some examples of innovative documentation display techniques and placements:

- Hang children's work or photographs on a suspended branch or old grapevine. Place the branch or vine in an unexpected location, such as over the children's cubbies or in the entrance hallway or lobby. You can hang the work along the branch horizontally or vertically. A branch or vine lends itself well to wire work (threading, wire sculptures, and so on) and to smaller photographic documentation pieces mounted on card stock for support and framing.

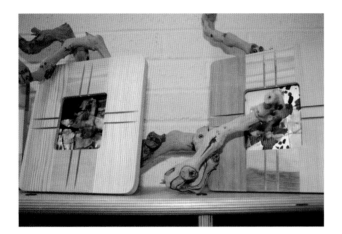 

- For ever-changing documentation, such as documentation of individual children's work, mount clipboards in rows or columns across a wall and easily add daily documentation on top of the previous days' work.

- Use the spokes of an umbrella (without fabric, upside down) for hanging documentation over areas where the documented event took place.

- Form freestanding display spaces by painting or covering large cardboard boxes in graduated sizes and then stacking the boxes. Mount documentation on this structure when wall space is not available. Or set it in a place where you know that foot traffic will be heavy, such as in an entrance hallway or lobby, and the work will garner attention.

- Amplify freestanding work such as a model or construction by setting it on a mirror tile or propping a large mirror behind the work.

- Use large old picture or window frames to contain several small documentation pieces. If frames are not available, make a grid out of lengths of bamboo tied together with natural string. Or make a large, simple frame of bamboo, and string lengths of wire or fishing line from one side to the other. Clip items onto these lengths of wire or line.

- If children have created many small pieces of work, or if you have a series of photographs you wish to place in a book, an accordion-style book will stand up along a shelf when opened. This type of book is easy for children and parents to examine together.

In this chapter, we have explored not only some possible ways to share documentation with families and the advantages of that sharing, but also how to draw attention to documentation. Following are some questions for you to consider about reaching out to families.

## INVITATION TO EXPLORE

- Consider your population. Given the cultural backgrounds and lifestyles of your families, what kinds of documentation would be the best fit for them? What would be your first step toward making your documentation more accessible to them?

- Choose a series of photographs that tell without words the story of a play session or event. How and where would you display these photos for the best possible effect? Write a concise account (one or two paragraphs) to put the photos in context and offer your reflections, and place this account nearby. What is the response from your families? What does this response tell you?

# 6

# Digital Documentation

Digital technology is developing at an astonishing pace. In some cases, it appears that we cannot manage our lives without it. So much technology exists to help educators create pedagogical documentation that it takes time, research, and networking with colleagues to discover all the tasks that technology can do for us. Using technology to create and share documentation has advantages as well as disadvantages. In this chapter, we will examine both.

## THE PROS

What are the advantages of electronic documentation? Practitioners who use digital means to engage in documentation often find that the speed and efficiency of this approach are attractive. There is no question that finding time for documentation is an issue for all of us. Additionally, educators find that communication with families is sometimes enhanced by this method. Let's take a closer look…

### Streamlining the Documentation Process

Of all the obstacles that educators face when trying to document children's work, simply finding the time is perhaps the most challenging. Among teachers I work with and support through teacher education and professional learning, the same comments and questions come up again and again in classes, workshops, and consultations: "I can see the value in this, but how will I find time to do it?" and "I do not get outside-of-class planning time, so how will I fit reflection and documentation into my day?"

Unlike most educators of older children, many early childhood educators do not get prep time, or paid time set aside solely for planning, reflection, and documentation. Of all the supports that administrators and supervisors could offer to their teachers, time to think and to document is one of the most valuable—but also one of the hardest to provide. So, how can technology help?

Many applications are available that enable us to take photographs and notes while we are observing children, both indoors and outdoors. For instance, Evernote or Pages downloaded onto a smartphone or tablet allows us to type in notes, add a photo or a short video, and save our work to a file designated for a particular child or classroom. We can then edit or expand these notes as needed and print them as short pieces of documentation.

Or for even more speed, we can use voice-to-text software. This software converts spoken language into written language, eliminating the need to type. Such applications sometimes misinterpret what has been said, with surprising or hilarious results! Careful editing is vital. However, voice-to-text software is getting smarter all the time. For instance, Voice Assistant uses intelligent speech recognition and learns from your past speech patterns. Other software choices include Dragon Dictation and Evernote, both of which can save audio and text together. This feature makes for an easier search when you are referring back to previously recorded data.

Donna Stapleton, executive director of Small World Learning Centre in Bridgewater, Nova Scotia, recently made the switch to digital documentation. She made the change after puzzling over how to help her staff solve the problem of having inadequate time for documentation. Following is her description of this transition.

In the past we used digital cameras and computers, and this took time, time, time (weekends, nights, lunchtime). I saw the value of portfolios and documentation, but also the stress of getting the work done efficiently. I wondered what we could do differently. One of our staff members and her husband are Mac users. They answered so many questions and showed us what was possible.

Now each teacher has an iPad mini. We are still learning about our iPads. We spend about ten minutes at our staff curriculum meeting each month sharing what we have learned, asking how to do certain things, and working through the transition together. This cooperation is a huge help, and our knowledge is growing.

With the iPad minis, staff can take photos or video or verbally record what is happening right on the spot. During naptime, staff members open up a Pages document, assemble the photo and text boxes, and size the items quickly by touch. They type or record their documentation. Some staff still take written notes as well.

At our staff reviews, all the staff members said they were able to create portfolios and documentation during their working day (at lunchtime or when numbers are low, as well as with the children), rather than taking this type of work home.

This month staff are meeting with parents for our regular parent-teacher dialogues. We will explain that we will soon start sending the children's portfolio pages home electronically every month. Staff can also include extra photos for particular parents as needed. This process will give our families a great resource to understand what their children are working on.

This short piece of documentation by one of Donna's staff shows the process that a child underwent as he watched fish in the classroom tank.

# Fishy Fishy In the Tank

H. was at the art table and he decided that he was going to draw the fish in the fish tank. He looked at the fish to see exactly what they looked like and what he might need to draw them. After close examination he found some brown paper and a pencil. After sitting down to start his drawing he said, "I need an orange crayon." He found the crayon and continued to draw. He paused for a moment and asked "Do I need to go this way Rhonda? I did this part but I forget what the tail looks like." He turned around and sat by the fish tank and looked at the tail while drawing. He finished drawing then cut out his fish. He smiled as he taped his fish to the outside of the tank. H. took his time and showed a great deal of concentration during this process.

Small World Learning Centre
Rhonda Smith
September 25th, 2013

Then, using this beginning piece, the teacher was able to step back and reflect:

> When reflecting on this first (electronic) on-the-spot documentation, I thought about trying to find out whether it was the fish itself that interested H., or the process of representing it. How was it possible to find out? I considered adding "real" items for representation in the art area, as an invitation. Would such items as natural materials, prints of paintings, and so on provoke a response in H.? Or, would it interest H. to make a 3-D representation of the fish, perhaps with clay? H.'s drawings are developing beyond simply basic shapes. He is looking carefully at all the parts of the fish and adding details. While watching the fish carefully, he was pointing out various parts, then remembering those parts when he came to actually drawing the fish.

What we see here is that although the documentation was quickly and electronically produced, it still provided an opportunity to revisit and examine H.'s process closely, to wonder about what was happening for him, to raise some questions, and to consider next steps.

## Encouraging Staff into the Documentation Process

When I have spoken with directors about how to engage their staff in documentation, they have reported that they sometimes encounter resistance. This resistance is mostly due to the shortage of time for documentation.

For teachers who are reluctant to take on this work, some directors find that digital technology can be a good entry point. Since younger staff members are likely to have grown up with lots of digital technology, this approach is comfortable for them. They are willing to "mess about" until they understand the process and can achieve their documentation goals efficiently.

Educators and philosophers David and Frances Hawkins proposed that children learn a tremendous amount from messing about with science and nature materials because this type of activity engages their natural curiosity. Architect Simon Nicholson's theory of loose parts suggests the same benefits from using open-ended materials: "In any environment, the degree of creativity and inventiveness is directly proportional to the number of variables in it" (1971, 30–34).

I think adults need to do this same kind of "messing about" when they are exploring any new idea or approach so that they understand and feel comfortable with all the variables and possibilities. Digital technology fits well into this framework. My early childhood education student teachers, for instance, have taught me much about electronic documentation through their absolute fearlessness. They mess about, share, experiment some more, and come up with innovative ways of solving minor glitches as well as creative ways of presenting children's work. Messing about engages their curiosity, and this leads to enthusiasm for exploring further.

## Efficient Sharing with Parents

When educators send home hard copies of classroom news, progress notes, pieces of documentation, and so on, many later find that their work has not been read. This is discouraging; teachers put much thought and time into this work for the express purpose of sharing with families. Educators also report that when the work goes home electronically, it is often read on smartphones and tablets, improving communication between school and home.

Many public schools, in fact, now send home only electronic report cards. Families then print out the report cards if they want hard copies. For parents who travel for work, for military families who are separated due to service demands, and in many other circumstances, electronic documentation is the only efficient way to share. In these situations, we often hear from family members who are heartened to be included in their children's school life.

## Design Opportunities

Even if you don't consider yourself to be particularly creative or knowledgeable in visual arts, digital technology can help you produce clean and tidy, professional-looking, creative layouts. One of the simplest approaches is to use an application such as PowerPoint to produce pages for portfolios, single sheets for extraordinary moments, or a series of sheets to be mounted together into panels. PowerPoint is so simple to use that many people do not need instruction. Rather, they simply open the program and explore, following their intuition, until they get the results they want. If trial and error doesn't do the trick, a simple tutorial or workshop is usually all that's needed to become efficient with PowerPoint and its many possibilities. PowerPoint provides design templates, backgrounds, typefaces, borders, and much more.

This image shows an example of a page from a documentation logbook. This PowerPoint page demonstrates a simple design, with the edges of the text and the photo aligned, and soft edges that blend into the color of the graphic design.

PowerPoint also provides photo-editing options such as resizing, fading edges, moving photos around the page, and so on. In my own work, PowerPoint has provided a simple, quick, and effective way to create a page each day for our logbook.

Microsoft Publisher also lends itself well to producing documentation. In particular, Publisher simplifies finding photographs from various locations, then storing them and manipulating them within documents.

## THE CONS

How can an approach that is accessible, streamlined, and fun to use have any disadvantages? Let's pause for a moment to remember the meaning and purpose of pedagogical documentation as outlined in earlier chapters:

Several pages created with PowerPoint are linked in order to revisit the story of a project with the children.

- It tells the story of learning, discussing children's ideas and theories while making them visible.

- It requires educators to reflect and carefully consider what was important for all the children involved in the event.

- It offers teachers the opportunity for learning because we must think deeply about the meaning of the child's work or words, what we can say about it, how to present it to others, and how we may respond to scaffold further exploration and learning. In addition, the questions that arise about children's thinking often lead to a deepened curiosity about the event, which in turns leads to further teacher research.

## Rushing the Process

With electronic documentation, we can—and often do—produce the work quickly. After all, speed is why many people use digital technology in the first place. However, we must remember that speed is not always conducive to reflection, that key pause during which we find meaning in the child's work and try to express why it is important. On-the-spot digital documentation may provide more quantity, but we must take care to maintain the quality of this work.

To maintain quality, we must use caution. We must remember why we are producing documentation in the first place. We should ask ourselves the following questions whenever we have produced on-the-spot documentation:

- Have we included traces of the children's ideas, thoughts, and questions? Even in the smallest piece of documentation, these traces add richness and context.

- Have we taken the time to think through what this event means? Have we captured the aha moment, or the long period of trial and error, or the joy of discovery? Have we expressed this in an articulate way for the reader or viewer?

- Is our "teacher thinking" evident? What are our questions? What do we wonder? What kind of research does this event lead us to?

## Privacy

Many of us have learned the hard way that when we share information electronically, we can't expect privacy. E-mails can go astray, people share passwords, web pages can be hacked, and so on. Therefore, we must discuss with families how we can protect their privacy and their children's privacy. We must decide what will be public and what will be private, and then strive to build and maintain these boundaries.

## SHARING DOCUMENTATION THROUGH SOCIAL MEDIA

After we have carefully considered and addressed our concerns about privacy and have family permissions in hand, we may find ourselves in a position to share some of our documentation through social media such as Facebook and Pinterest. Some people use these sites at first in a purely social way but later develop professional pages. That is, they share no personal information, and their messages pertain only to the professional side of their lives. A professional early childhood education Pinterest collection, for instance, might contain only boards that pertain to early learning, pedagogical documentation, provocations and invitations, interesting publications, learning environments, and so on. Through perusing such a collection, it is easy to ascertain its creator's philosophy and perspective and explore further by linking to sites that have inspired this person.

It is exciting to think about the sharing opportunities that social media offers. For a teacher, the main advantage of such sharing is the opportunity to learn from other teachers. We may be inspired by the wording they use to describe children's work or by the graphic design they use to illustrate an event. When we find a person or early childhood education setting whose work excites and inspires us, we can continue to follow that person's work. For example, I have discovered stunning documentation through Pinterest, contacted the people who created it through the information they provided, and phoned them to have a conversation and learn more about their work. Some of their work appears in this book. We can also follow colleagues whose work we admire but whose location precludes face-to-face contact.

On their blog *Technology-Rich Inquiry-Based Research,* Canadian educators Diane Kashin and Louise Jupp share their views on this type of sharing through social media. In their article "The Three Stages of Curation," they suggest that these stages consist of collecting and collating, condensing and contextualizing, and creating and critiquing.

The authors go on to suggest that "when digital curation is used as a professional learning research process, the second stage of curation needs to be considered. Here it helps to consider the need to condense *and* contextualize. At this stage of research our thought process involves the consideration of how we might add value to our digital research data" (2013).

Jupp and Kashin suggest that the final stage—creation and critique—is both challenging and rewarding. They say that "the principles of Making Learning Visible are a guidepost here. Diane [Kashin] and I give thoughtful consideration, in conversation with each other, to the images we post on our blog, the quotes we use, and the insights offered. Our Facebook page is a very public social media tool we utilize to engage community participation in our research. . . . [It] has a built-in provocation to comment. On a larger scale, the development of a blog creates context" (2013).

There is no end to the professional networks that are available online. We simply have to search, find the right fit for our own circumstances, philosophies, and beliefs, and make the connections. These connections may be in the next county over or on the other side of the world. This ability to share ideas with anyone anywhere is one of the great joys of electronic networking.

## DEVELOPING A WEBSITE OR BLOG

To share your documentation and other aspects of your work more fully, consider building a professional website or blog. Many online platforms guide users through the creation of their own websites or blogs. They are accessible, easy to use, and affordable (often free). They are a common choice for many early childhood settings and professionals.

### Creating a Professional Blog

If you are using a blog for sharing your documentation efforts, it might include documentation that explains such aspects as the following:

- the originating idea for the children's work

- how the work unfolded

- what children had to say about the work, or for nonverbal children, how they interacted with materials, other children, and adults

- how this work affected your own thinking or teaching practice. What questions did this work raise for you?

One of the most intriguing aspects of blogging is that you can allow readers to post comments in response to your work. In this way, a conversation evolves among you and your readers. Learning occurs on all sides of this conversation.

If you want to build your own blog, be sure to form a plan that will let you create a high-quality blog in the time you have. What makes a high-quality blog? I have discussed this with educators who follow certain early childhood education blogs that address documentation and inquiry. These educators made the following points:

- Seeing photographs of stunning work by children does not help us grow or think if we do not understand the context, the children's ideas, and the teachers' thinking about the events that unfolded. So a good blog will describe, often by sharing documentation, the meaning behind the shared work.

- A high-quality blog is updated regularly. Each time readers check in, they find something new to think about or explore.

- A good blog is easy to navigate. Information is appropriately labeled with headings, the blog is designed for clarity, and it is pleasing to the eye. It attracts the reader.

Over time and with enough exploration, you will probably find a few blogs that become favorites of yours. Perhaps you will find documentation that tells the story of a teacher's journey with inquiry and documentation, and this may speak to your own experiences. Or perhaps a teacher's documentation will echo moments with children that you have engaged in, struggled with, or aspired to. Whatever the reason for your interest, you can bookmark or subscribe to updates from these blogs for easy, regular access to their information. Over time, a relationship can form between you, the blogger, and the blogger's other readers.

At the time of publication, some of my own favorites include the following:

- TransformEd (www.myclassroomtransformation.blogspot.ca)

- Irresistible Ideas for Play Based Learning (www.playbasedlearning.com.au)

- Journey into Early Childhood (www.journeyintoearlychildhood.weebly.com)

- Technology-Rich Inquiry-Based Research (tecribresearch.wordpress.com)

## How Does a Website Differ from a Blog?

A blog is a type of magazine, with the blogger as the editor or publisher. A blog offers the opportunity to post frequent articles on ever-changing topics and to receive responses to those articles. As with websites, search engines will crawl your blog regularly to help potential readers find updated material. Blogs are cheap or free to produce, although upkeep can take a lot of time. As a blogger, you can present your work informally if you like.

Websites, on the other hand, are more like digital storefronts. The main pages of a website are somewhat permanent. The main pages of an early childhood education website, for example, might contain basic information about the owner of the site and this person's work and philosophy. Other pages of the website, which may include a blog, can be changed more easily.

Which digital platform you use to share your work, especially your documentation of that work, will depend on several factors:

- The time you have available to maintain and update the work: Both need frequent updates in order for search engines to bring them up when a reader is searching for specific information. However, blog followers tend to expect regular and frequent updates from the writer.

- Whether you are sharing work in the context of your early childhood education setting: You may want to create a website to share permanent information about the setting or a philosophy and embed a blog within that site to share changing documentation about project work.

- How much money your budget allows you to spend: Website designer fees vary widely. You can, of course, design your own site if you are technologically confident.

- How much information you wish to post: A website can be designed to handle many pages of photographs, graphics, and text because it's created to meet your specific needs. Blogs vary in capacity, so it is important to investigate how much information a blog can contain before you commit to it.

Website designer Belinda Naugler Adams offers the following advice: "A tight budget is often the main factor that leads people to consider a do-it-yourself website. Although this option appears attractive at first, a professional designer will understand how to build your site using a wide array of best practices and proven strategies to ensure that your site performs as intended and ranks highly in searches for maximum online success. In today's business climate, your online presence is a vital part of your business. Entrusting your online presence to a poorly designed, ineffective website is a recipe for failure. Your website must be as professional as you are."

## INVITATION TO EXPLORE

- Produce a small piece of documentation using a publishing application. Compare this to documentation that you have produced in a more traditional way. What are the differences and similarities between the two pieces? What are the strengths and challenges of each approach?

- Search for and explore some blogs that share documentation and that you think might connect to your own philosophy. Think critically about the content. What are the strengths of these blogs? Where do they fall short? In what ways might they support your practice?

# 7

# Reflections

When we consider all the examples of pedagogical documentation offered in the previous chapters, we can see that this work takes us on a journey. Through documentation, we move from

- describing the children's work, to

- reflecting on what it might mean, to

- considering the possibilities for response, to

- responding in ways that involve the hearts and minds of both children and teachers.

This kind of deep thinking and engagement is what keeps us passionate about our work over the long term. I cannot imagine having worked with young children for more than thirty years if I had not had the opportunity to think with them—to engage in the delight of discovery with them, to watch their faces as understanding dawns, to learn from them and alongside them, and to make that learning visible so that others might share and understand it.

Whether the children in our care are young toddlers or school-age children, their work shown back to them profoundly influences their self-esteem, confidence, and thinking. We educators need only learn to take note of, reflect on, and revisit the work with the children in order to think along with them. And when we think in this manner, we inevitably come up with questions. What do we do with these questions? Teacher research offers a way for us to explore our questions through our practice.

## DOCUMENTATION AS TEACHER RESEARCH

What is teacher research, and how might it affect our day-to-day lives in the classroom? Andrew Stremmel, a professor at South Dakota State University, specializes in teacher inquiry and uses Reggio-inspired, inquiry-based approaches to early childhood teacher education. He provides a clear and simple definition of teacher research:

When teachers begin to pursue their teaching questions, using methods that are meaningful to them for the purpose of improving their teaching and children's learning, they engage in teacher research. Teacher research is practice-focused inquiry. Teachers' research questions emerge from areas they consider problematic (i.e., puzzling, intriguing, astonishing) or from issues they simply want to know more about. (Stremmel 2012)

Since teacher research usually begins with a question that we would like to answer, we must think about how to formulate that question. Stremmel says that this can be challenging, and he suggests discussion with a trusted colleague: "Together, pondering and discussing your interests, wonderings, and curiosities can lead to great insights and new understandings" (2012).

I propose that documentation, too, can lead us to questions, wonderings, and new understandings. And I think that discussing photographs and transcripts of children in action before constructing the documentation provides the best results. Conversation with trusted peers together with concrete data describing what children have been doing often make meaning or understanding easier to achieve. Such discussions also inevitably raise further questions, which we can attempt to answer through our practice, and so the cycle of inquiry continues.

As we all know, however, teachers get sidetracked easily when we gather to discuss ideas and practice. We are sometimes starved for collegial discussion, and this may lead our discussions astray. We may find a solution to this problem in Ben Mardell and Andrée Howard's article "Inquiry as a Team Sport, in which the authors share their experiences with a peer network. The members of this network meet regularly at one another's centers to discuss ideas, perspectives, and understandings. Mardell and Howard describe how a peer network uses documentation along with a protocol in which one teacher presents her documentation, poses a question, and then listens:

> The protocol asks participants to separate what they observe from their interpretations and suggestions. The protocol begins with teachers constructing collective meaning from the documentation. Participants describe their own observations regarding the situation presented. Each person brings a unique perspective and will notice something different. Then the other teachers give suggestions, which are often richer after the close examination of the documentation. Second, the presenting teacher is in listening mode most of the time. After she presents the context and poses a question, she listens. (Mandell and Howard 2012, 13)

Having used this type of protocol in my own practice, I can attest to the fact that it does keep participants on track in terms of discussing the documentation at hand, and it encourages participants to develop fuller and richer documentation to share. Listening to others' interpretations of one's work is a valuable learning experience. In the case of documentation, this exercise makes clear what is understood (or not understood) and how our work is interpreted.

## A Student Teacher's Research Experience

As I am writing this book, Aya is a second-year student at the Nova Scotia College of Early Childhood Education. Aya is interested in documentation as a means to understanding children's thinking and learning. At times, documentation has helped her understand how children construct knowledge. In the following documentation, we see the deep thinking and learning that Aya underwent as she examined photographs of children struggling with 3-D and 2-D representation.

**Journal: How Do Children Come to Understand 3-D?**
**Date: November 15, 2013**

In the studio, child T was working on making a house using clay, sticks, and other materials. He looked at pictures of an apartment building and made an umbrella on the top of the building, as in the illustration, using a stick and a gear-shaped item. He then put a rectangle block next to it. For him, the block is one of the windows in the building. (He pointed to one window on the fourth floor.)

The other child, child M, made a house using wood branches, as shown in the following picture. He looked at a picture of a house and used the sticks as walls, a roof, and a chimney. He even added a gear on the top of the chimney and called it a fan for the chimney.

I learned how children see and think of 3-D objects. Some children pay attention to details, and some of them make 2-D representations like child M did. I previously thought that it might help children to give them a box to make a house, but this experience gave me ideas that asking children to actually build a 3-D object could be really helpful for children to understand 3-D. If I give them a box to make a house, it will be hard to see how children struggle to understand 3-D objects. But if they process their thoughts through their own way of making 3-D objects, I can then see how much they understand, and it will help me to help them build a better understanding.

Next, intrigued and puzzled by her questions about how children learn about 3-D, Aya offered a 3-D puzzle to her children, with the following results:

### Journal: How Do Children Come to Understand 3-D?
### Date: November 21, 2013

I offered 3-D block puzzles that had different-shaped block pieces that made a 3 × 3 × 3 cube when put together in a certain way. I brought pictures of many possible combinations made from these pieces, so children could see what the assembled puzzles should look like. Each block piece has a single color. Children seemed to have some difficulty seeing the 2-D pictures as 3-D objects. They had a hard time figuring out how to use the picture to create a 3 × 3 × 3 cube. Some of them ignored the image and kept trying to connect the different pieces. Some children put all the pieces on the picture so the colors matched, but then realized that this strategy does not make a cube.

I helped them see the blocks from one view, so that it looks like the picture. Children had a hard time seeing the connection, but once I took a *photo* of the pattern together with their arrangement, they realized that theirs did not look like what they wanted to make. They then changed the position of the blocks, and I took pictures again. They looked at the pictures and changed again until they found that it was right! In this process they made a 3-D object, which I made into 2-D (a photo) so they could compare what they did in 3-D to the 2-D pattern shown on the guide.

Taking pictures of what they did in 3-D space may help them to understand what a 3-D object really looks like as a 2-D picture. At the end, three children could create the cube with my help (asking questions when they made a mistake).

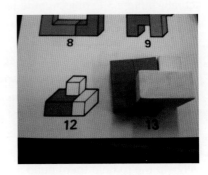

Child M said he had successfully made shape number twelve using blocks. Child M didn't change his mind until he saw this photo. He then changed the shape and said that this time it was just like number twelve. He saw this photo and realized that there was something wrong.

This is what he made at the end. He looked at the photo and smiled.

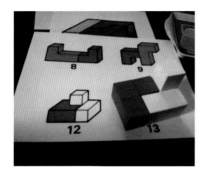 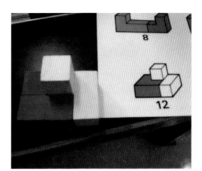

These pieces of documentation, outlining Aya's question as well as the child's struggles, enable Aya to see constructivism in action. They also allow her to see how to answer her own questions about children's thinking and learning. We see her reflection that simply giving children a cardboard box will not help them build their own understanding of 3-D. She offers a different material, which encompasses both 2-D and 3-D shapes, for the children to manipulate. But then, seeing the struggle continue, she takes her scaffolding to the next step. She provides photographs (2-D representations) as documentation of what the children have actually built for them to revisit and consider. A teacher's question—"How do children learn about 3-D shapes?"—is answered through the use of careful thinking together with documentation that can be examined with the child.

## More Teachers' Questions

At Garden Gate Child Development Center in Vineyard Haven, Massachusetts, Leigh Ann Yuen and her colleagues have been watching and taking note of the toddlers in their care. Leigh Ann's work is inspired by the practices of Reggio Emilia, and her documentation reflects the thinking of the children and the teachers, using a refined aesthetic expression.

For an example of how documentation supported Leigh Ann and her colleagues in sustaining toddlers' expression of their thinking, as well as the questions that the toddlers' play generated for teachers, let's look at how her toddlers engaged in an exploration of horses and spinning, provoked by their intimate knowledge of a local carousel. Leigh Ann explains in her reflection how this journey began. Notice that throughout her reflection, questions arise for the teachers. How are these questions addressed through practice?

The Flying Horses Carousel is a historic landmark in our community. It is the nation's oldest platform carousel, and it is a rite of passage for all children growing up on Martha's Vineyard to ride the carousel and ultimately grab the brass ring, the coveted prize that earns its holder a free ride. So it came as no surprise to me and my coteacher when the children began to play out this beloved ride in their dramatic play. One of the two-and-a-half-year-olds instructed her friends to "pick a horse" and then sent them off, saying, "Thank you and enjoy your ride!" in perfect imitation of the local high-schoolers who run the carousel all summer.

We observed this play over several days as more of the toddlers in our group realized what was going on in the dramatic play area. We offered a roll of tickets and a basket of wooden rings from the block area, and the play continued. My coteacher and I were curious. In addition to the obvious fun factor, what was it about the carousel that kept these children engaged in this play, day after day? The play continued outside with the children setting up chairs in the music garden next to the big bell, which sounds so much like the bell that signals the start of the carousel ride. As we documented the children's play, we noticed their desire to imitate the carousel experience exactly. They wanted the horses, the tickets, the music, and the rings. The only thing their imaginary carousel didn't do was spin! We sent out wish lists to parents and scoured the local thrift shop for things that spin. We searched for lazy Susans to add to the block area, thinking that some children might be interested in building carousels that really spun. A lucky donation of a basket full of toy horses completed the provocation, and we were eager to see how the children would use these new materials. The lazy Susans were a big hit and were immediately put to use by every child in turn. In our observations, we saw that the horses were seldom used with the spinner, but blocks, race cars, toy people, and more were carefully arranged, then spun at varying speeds until they blurred into a colorful loop. Spinning itself became the focus of our inquiry.

We took the children outside and invited them to explore spinning with their bodies. We took our lazy Susans into the studio to explore the mechanics of spinning with paint and markers. We pushed the limits with giant spin art on a bicycle tire.

In the meantime, some children had discovered the basket of horses, and an inquiry began exploring the similarities and differences between real horses and carousel horses. A few of our children were interested in exploring the differences in the studio and chose to create carousel horses with markers, glue, and glitter. By this time, the Flying Horses Carousel

Spinning offers children a sense of exuberance, of freedom. Spinning, getting dizzy, and regaining balance helps children orient themselves in space. The development of the vestibular system results in balanced and coordinated movement. When the children were first asked about things that spin, their first response was, "Me! I spin!!"

As children spend time engaged in these kinds of movement activities, they explore the concept of spinning with their whole bodies. What does everything look like when you are spinning? What do you hear? How does your body feel? These are questions we will be exploring in the children's play.

The children have spent a great deal of time investigating how our spinning objects work. Through engineering inquiry in the classroom and in the studio, the children have begun to develop their own ideas and theories about spinning.

"It works. You spin it round." -Jake

"It's a track. I just put a car on it and then it spins." -Dejana

"Fast, so fast! Faster! Faster! - Angus

"My hand makes it go and my hand makes it stop." -Silas

"It's a spinner. It spins. [What makes it spin?] Maybe the stripes? Oh! Maybe this part—a screw!" -Sienna

"There's a little tiny button." -Dejana      "It is a button." -Silas

had closed for the winter. The children were no longer interested in playing out this idea in dramatic play, but they remained interested in the carousel itself. It was the fanciful, colorful, whimsical horses of the carousel that held the interest of our horse lovers.

Three months in, we were still trying to answer the question, What is it about the Flying Horses that has captured the children so completely? We invited the toddlers to draw the Flying Horses. One of the toddlers eagerly started to draw, creating a rapid, spiraling

October 2012

## Round and Round and Round and

The children's interest in the dramatic play of The Flying Horses, led us to observations of their interest in all things that go round and round! What makes The Flying Horses so much fun? The horses, the music, the brass rings, sure. But the real fun comes in the *ride!*

Most kids know what it feels like to spin and spin until they're dizzy, falling down and laughing and doing it again. The kids in the Little Room are practicing balance and developing their vestibular system. They're also exploring the effects of spinning on objects.

The addition of a "lazy susan" in the block area caught the attention of many and an investigation of things that spin was begun!

drawing, and proudly announced, "Around! Okay! Do you want to see me draw 'around'?" Another child quickly added, "It spins all around!" Other children drew series of brass rings. And some refined their drawings of horses, using references from the computer to enhance their work. It is the details that the children were trying to capture. They were trying to re-create the carousel to make it their own. Their relationship with the carousel is an intimate one. This is a dear, familiar friend, a source of excitement and joy, and the children were seeking companionship.

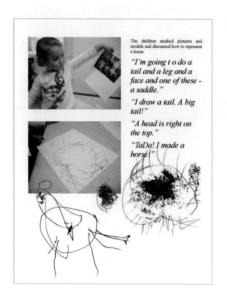

The children studied pictures and models and discussed how to represent a horse.

"I'm going t o do a tail and a leg and a face and one of these - a saddle."

"I draw a tail. A big tail!"

"A head is right on the top."

"TaDa! I made a horse!"

"The horses!"    "I'm gonna draw the horse!"

"I'm gonna draw the horses. But I don't know how to draw a horse!!!"

We went back to the computer to look for references for drawing horses. We typed in 'horse' and found several pictures of horses on a farm, in a field, etc.

"No. These are different."

Then we typed in 'carousel horse'.

"Yeah! These are exactly what I'm talking about!"

The children are beginning to distinguish between real and make-believe. They can recognize the differences between actual horses and the fanciful horses on the carousel.

"The pink one! I want the pink one!"

Spring arrived, and with it the reopening of the Flying Horses Carousel. The children quickly agreed that a field trip to the carousel was in order. Our documentation of this trip had two goals. The first was to record all the fine details of the carousel itself: the antique horses with horsehair manes, the 1923 Wurlitzer band organ that plays tunes on original paper rolls, the white picket fence that keeps all the children eagerly waiting. The second goal was to record the children's interactions with the carousel: their anticipa-

# Can you draw the Flying Horses?

"Around! Ok, do you want to see me draw 'around'?"

"It spins all around!"

The children now have a deep understanding of 'around'. These two children have made the connection between their experiences on the carousel and their experiences with spinning in the classroom. When invited to draw a picture of the flying horses, they are able to express the concept visually on their paper and are satisfied with their representation of the carousel's thrilling motion.

"And these are fast, right? They really go really fast."

tion in waiting for a horse, their excitement as the starting bell rings, their delight as the ride picks up speed.

Throughout the project, our documentation was accessible to the children. Displayed in the classroom alongside the children's artistic interpretations of the carousel, the project documentation prompted questions and conversations about the carousel. But it was this new documentation of the carousel itself that provoked intense dialogue and drew all the children back into the project 100 percent. The documentation became a new voice in our midst. Some of the children, surprisingly, responded with uneasiness or apprehension. They said the music had been too loud, or the ride had spun too fast. They pointed out the picture of the organ or the relatively reassuring bench seats where some of them had snuggled in their parents' laps. When we invited these children to join the others in creating our own model of the carousel, they agreed, but they held tight to the documentation to help them articulate their own needs and desires in its construction.

It became clear to us that each of the children had a deep emotional bond with the carousel. In creating our model, the children returned time and time again to the documentation to check the details, to represent the carousel with the accuracy of their imaginations, to blend their reality with their fantasy. This was the answer to our question; this was the real reason the play persisted. The Flying Horses Carousel was an established play-mate. The consistency of its details was a comfort to the young children who encountered it time and time again, and the magic of the ride was of their own making.

Leigh Ann's explanation of how the project evolved, meandering among several interests connected to the carousel and how it connected reality to fantasy, demonstrates how documentation supports ongoing deep exploration. She explains this process from the teachers' point of view:

Our documentation throughout this project, from October to April and beyond, helped us as teachers frame questions about the children's play; evaluate strategies for deepening exploration; engage in meaningful conversations with children, parents, and other teachers; and extend the project work over several months' time. As a result, we gained greater insight into the emotional lives of our children.

Here, in bulleted form, is how Leigh Ann sees the role documentation played throughout this investigation:

- Documentation was begun in the first place to explore the children's compelling interest in the carousel.

- Documentation of the children's initial dramatic play illustrated the lack of spinning in their imaginary carousel.

- Documentation of play with lazy Susans led teachers in a new direction, exploring the mechanics of spinning.

- Documentation of the children's play with horses returned our thoughts to the carousel project and highlighted the children's interest in fantasy thinking.

- Documentation of children's drawings of the Flying Horses illustrated the children's interests in the details of the carousel and the differences between real and fantasy horses.

- Documentation of the field trip to the Flying Horses Carousel became a powerful communication tool for children and teachers.

Within this list, we can see how the documentation made visible the spiral effect of scaffolding. The children moved from the carousel to spinning to horses to exploring fantasy and reality, then back to the carousel for a visit to the real place where the whole exploration began. Throughout, the documentation helped focus and clarify the teachers' thinking and responses, sometimes leading them to pause and reflect once more and to develop more questions about the children's intentions.

Some people outside our profession may question whether very young children can engage in such deep exploration, yet documentation shows that indeed they can. Documentation makes children's competence visible and strengthens our image of them.

## THE PEDAGOGY OF LISTENING

"The pedagogy of listening," a phrase coined by Carlina Rinaldi, president of Reggio Children and professor of pedagogy at the University of Modena and Reggio Emilia, may at first lead us to think about listening in the traditional, familiar sense; that is, we listen to what we hear. But Rinaldi takes us further than that. She defines listening in a much broader and deeper sense. In her article "The Pedagogy of Listening: The Listening Perspective from Reggio Emilia" (2001), Rinaldi describes the many meanings of listening:

- a way of connecting to others

- listening with all our senses

- recognizing the many ways in which people use varied languages, symbols, and codes to express themselves

- internal listening

- listening generated by curiosity, desire, doubt, and uncertainty

- listening as producing questions rather than answers

- listening as giving an interpretation

- listening as the basis for any learning relationship

As I read this list of definitions of listening, I was drawn to the many connections between Rinaldi's descriptions of listening and the ways in which documentation enables us to listen to children. When we are documenting, for instance,

- we connect with children,

- we recognize the many ways in which they express themselves (their languages),

- we are filled with curiosity, desire, and sometimes doubt,

- we produce questions in response to our intense listening,

- we try to interpret, and

- our careful listening deepens our relationships with children.

Rinaldi goes on to say:

> In addition to offering support and mediation to the children, the teacher who knows how to observe, document and interpret these processes will realize his or her own full potential as a learner—in this case, learning how to teach. Documentation can be seen as visible listening: it ensures listening and being listened to by others. (Rinaldi 2001)

Documentation at its best is a process that spirals upward to higher forms of listening, thinking, and learning for all the people involved. It begins with the children, then moves to the teachers as we respond to the children's work with interest, questions, and careful observation. It moves back again to the children, as teachers explore with them, looking for meaning and co-constructing knowledge through further conversations or invitations to action. Then the teachers engage in more thinking, as we try to construct visible traces of the work. Then the process moves outward to families or colleagues, as we share the children's and teachers' thinking and actions. Perhaps it moves back to teachers and children again, as we gather responses from readers of the documentation. What have they heard us say? What have they understood?

Documentation is not a simple process. Yet it has the power to sustain and inspire us and to support the growth of everyone who is involved with it—the children who begin the process, their families who share in the work, and the teachers who work so hard and think so deeply in order to make it all happen. Pedagogical documentation is collaborative, and we all share in its rewards of fulfillment, understanding, and continued growth.

## INVITATION TO EXPLORE

As you travel further on your documentation journey, here are some questions to consider as starting points in deciding what to document:

- What do you wonder? That is, what do you find puzzling, intriguing, surprising, or just plain interesting? How will you present these intriguing events or thoughts to others?

- How will you use documentation as a part of your own learning? Do you have questions and some hypotheses about teaching and learning that you can make visible through documentation of your teacher research?

- Where will you begin your documentation journey?

# Glossary

**collaboration:** During an inquiry, collaboration is an essential working together that occurs between children and adults, parents and school, children and children. Collaboration supports the construction of knowledge, with input from all the participants.

**emergent curriculum:** An inquiry-based way of teaching and learning that begins with observations, then moves to reflections, thoughtful responses, and more observation in order to co-construct a curriculum with children in a way that is based on collaboration. Intentional, creative, and thoughtful curriculum emerges from interactions among all the protagonists in the classroom.

**hundred languages:** A term that originated with Loris Malaguzzi in Reggio Emilia, referring to the many ways in which children might express their knowledge and views of the world. For instance, children may best express their thoughts through drama, music, graphic arts, speech, and so on.

**hypotheses:** The children's understandings and ideas about why something is occurring, or their educated guesses at what might happen next. A child's hypothesis represents her understanding of her world at a given moment in time.

**inquiry:** In the context of emergent curriculum, inquiry refers to the circular process that occurs when teachers observe, reflect, respond to children, offer invitations to scaffold learning, then observe and reflect again. An inquiry may last for days or for months, depending on the level of interest and engagement from all involved.

**intentionality:** Having a specific purpose in mind; being purposeful in one's actions with and for children.

**missing middle:** A term to express the (sometimes missing) pause for reflection upon what we have seen and heard in the classroom.

**pedagogical documentation:** A way of making children's and teachers' thinking and learning visible. Pedagogical documentation consists of records of the collaboration between children and teachers during their learning journeys. This record can be a powerful communication tool between children and teachers, families and school, colleagues, and the public. Pedagogical documentation also provides a means for reflective practice on the part of the teacher, often raising questions about teaching and learning.

**pedagogista:** An Italian term for the person who works with school systems in a role of curriculum coordinator and resource person, and who collaborates closely with teachers. A pedagogista engages in dialogue and reflection with teachers, parents, and other colleagues on topics such as possible projects, teacher development and training, and directions for future work with children.

**project:** A long- or short-term project is the investigation undertaken by small or large groups of children on a topic of interest to them. In collaboration with one another, children and teachers engage in in-depth exploration, activities, and representations of their understanding.

**rationale:** The reason for proceeding with a particular course of action or for holding a belief. Possession of a sound rationale helps to ensure that the adults engaged with children are intentional in their practice.

**reflection:** As used in this book, reflection refers to the deep thinking involved before responding to children's actions and words. Reflection provides a lens through which we examine children's work closely, looking for underlying meanings, patterns, understandings, and misunderstandings. Reflection can be undertaken alone or with colleagues.

**scaffolding:** Taken from the work of Lev Vygotsky, this term refers to the supports offered to children—by teachers or a more experienced peer—to help them take their understanding to a higher level. It provides for constructivist learning, in that children are able to move forward in their understanding at their own pace in a safe and nurturing learning environment.

**schema:** A way of categorizing and organizing knowledge that is part of intellectual growth. For children, as new knowledge is gained, old schemas are adjusted or changed.

# References

Carter, Margie and Deb Curtis. 2010. *The Visionary Director: A Handbook for Dreaming, Organizing, and Improvising in Your Center,* Second Edition. Saint Paul, MN: Redleaf Press.

Jupp, Louise. 2013. "Documentation and Assessment: The Power of a Learning Story." *Technology-Rich Inquiry-Based Research* (blog). http://tecribresearch.wordpress.com/2013/04/24/documentation-and-assessment-the-power-of-a-learning-story-10/.

Jupp, Louise and Diane Kashin. 2013. "Three Stages of Curation." *Technology-Rich Inquiry-Based Research blog.* http://tecribresearch.wordpress.com/2013/02/12/three-stages-of-curation/.

Lewin-Benham, Ann. 2011. *Twelve Best Practices for Early Childhood Education: Integrating Reggio and Other Inspired Approaches.* New York: Teachers College Press.

Malaguzzi, Loris. 1993. "For an Education Based on Relationships." *Young Children* 49 (1).

Mardell, Ben, and Andrée Howard. 2012. "Inquiry as a Team Sport." *Voices of Practitioners* 7 (1).

Nicholson, Simon. 1971. "How Not to Cheat Children: The Theory of Loose Parts." *Landscape Architecture* 62 (1): 30–34.

Project Zero. 2003. *Making Teaching Visible: Documenting Individual and Group Learning as Professional Development.* Cambridge, MA: Project Zero, Harvard Graduate School of Education.

Rinaldi, Carlina. 2001. "The Pedagogy of Listening: The Listening Perspective from Reggio Emilia." *Innovations.* Vol. 8, no. 4, Fall 2001.

Stacey, Susan. 2009. *Emergent Curriculum in Early Childhood Settings: From Theory to Practice.* Saint Paul, MN: Redleaf Press.

Stremmel, Andrew. 2012. "Finding a Research Question." *Voices of Practitioners* 7 (1).

Wien, Carol Anne, Victoria Guyevskey, and Noula Berdoussis. 2011. "Learning to Document in Reggio-Inspired Education." *Early Childhood Research & Practice* 13 (2).

# Index